Monarch

C0-AOH-020

Miami Cycle & Mfg. Co.

HARLEY-DAVIDSON

Excelsior

Thor

EXCELSIOR CYCLE
MOTOR MFG. AUTO SIOR AND SUPPLY

PIERCE

FLANDERS "4"

"Motorette"

MATCHLESS MOTOR.

RUDGE WHITWORTH
COVENTRY

CLYDE

Champion

Brough Superior

THE FLYING MERKEL

THE HOLLEY

Michaelson

EXCELSIOR
EXCELSIOR MOTOR Co
BIRMINGHAM

THE JAMES

The Kenzler-Waverley

NER·A·CAR

OTO GUZZI

FN

AJS

PIRATE

De Luxe

ROYAL ENFIELD

DAVID GLENN HUNT
MEMORIAL LIBRARY
GALVESTON COLLEGE

Motorcycle Pioneers

The Men, the Machines, the Events 1860~1930

Illustrations and text by **Michael Partridge**

DAVID GLENN HUNT
MEMORIAL LIBRARY
GALVESTON COLLEGE

Arco Publishing Company, Inc.

New York

Published 1977 by Arco Publishing Company, Inc.
219 Park Avenue South, New York, N.Y. 10003

Copyright © 1976 by Michael Partridge

All rights reserved

Printed in Great Britain

Library of Congress Cataloging in Publication Data
Partridge, Michael.
  Motorcycle pioneers.
  Bibliography: p.
  1. Motorcycles—History. 2. Motorcycle
racing—History. I. Title.
TL440.P26   629.22'75'09034   76-12553
ISBN 0-668-04035-1

Contents

Foreword 4
Introduction 6
Hildebrand and Wolfmuller motorcycle 16
1¾hp De Dion-Bouton motor tricycle 18
Four-cylinder Holden motorcycle 24
¾hp Werner motorcycle 26
222cc Singer Motorwheel 28
2½hp Clyde motorcycle 30
2hp Werner motorcycle 32
2¾hp Excelsior motorcycle 34
2¾hp Quadrant motorcycle 36
3hp Harley Davidson motorcycle 38
3½hp Phelon & Moore Forecar 40
2½hp Joseph Barter motorcycle 42
3hp Triumph motorcycle 44
944cc NLG Peugeot motorcycle 46
Vindec Special motorcycle 48
500cc FN motorcycle 50

2¾hp Douglas Model K motorcycle 52
3hp Pearson-Cox steam bicycle 54
3½hp Matchless TT motorcycle 56
1hp Wall Autowheel 58
3½hp Scott motorcycle 60
976cc BAT motorcycle 62
350cc Elswick motorcycle 64
11hp American Militaire motorcycle 66
3½hp Rudge Multi motorcycle 68
1¾hp Autoped scooter 70
5/6hp Clyno-Vickers machine-gun combination 72
Sunbeam motorcycle 74
500cc Indian Powerplus motorcycle 76
1hp ABC Skootamota 78
1,000cc Daytona motorcycle 80
500cc Brough Flat-twin 82
2½hp Autoglider 84

490cc SV Norton motorcycle 86
3½hp NUT motorcycle 88
350cc Pullin-Groome motorcycle 90
1½hp Alvis auto-scooter 92
2½hp Levis motorcycle 94
1¾hp Grigg scooter 96
2¾hp Ner-a-Car 98
2¾hp AJS motorcycle 100
500cc Rudge dirt-track motorcycle 102
500 cc Douglas dirt-track motorcycle 104
500cc Moto Guzzi motorcycle 106
500cc Cotton-Blackburne Special sprint racing motorcycle 108
1,000cc Brough superior racing combination 110
Acknowledgements 112
Bibliography 112

Foreword

It may come as a surprise to those who marvel at the weird and wonderful motorcycles illustrated in this book that many of them do still exist and, thanks to improved oils and fuels, can now perform with more vigour than ever. Not only can many be viewed in various museums, but some are still to be seen in action in road runs and rallies.

This happy state of affairs is due more to the efforts of a few enthusiasts than to foresight on the part of the motorcycle industry which more or less overlooked the need to preserve a 'living' record of its achievements. This was very much the attitude of a forward-looking generation—life was short and exciting in its developments with no time for nostalgia. The few veteran machines hoarded by their manufacturers were mostly swept away by constant financial disasters or lost during the wars.

One factor which ensured the safety of veteran machines was the organising by the Sunbeam Motor Cycle Club, of an annual London-to-Brighton run for machines built before 1914.

Post-1914 machines did not enjoy this 'protection' and, being just 'old bikes', were scrapped or left to rot away. There are so many vintage machines (built between 1914 and 1930) around today because many owners were too lazy to clear out their rubbish or too sentimental to part with an old friend. It was possible for old motorcycles to lie about for years. The World War II scrap metal shortage decimated the ranks of old motorcycles but also created nostalgia for days gone by when, starved of new development enthusiasts began to look backward to find interest in veteran models, or rediscover the performance and simplicity of vintage models.

The Vintage Motorcycle Club was formed in 1946 and has become one of the biggest in the world and the recognized authority on all matters appertaining to motorcycles of more than twenty-five years old. In this way the Club ensures that history is served by a continuous process of preservation. Times change as do the machines in use by members, but the Club remains dedicated to its original creed . . .

. . . united by the common appreciation of the engineering skill and vision of those who built the pioneer motorcycles but, moreover, determined that such machines are not preserved as lifeless exhibits in a museum, but are brought to life on frequent occasions in order that a new generation can marvel at the handiwork of the pioneers and an older generation can once again view with nostalgia the machines they rode in days gone by.

This creed has resulted in the recreation of the vintage and veteran scene through runs, rallies and even road races and reliability trials, so that a Rip Van Winkle might wake at a Vintage Club meet to find little had changed.

Vintage enthusiasts, young and old, will, I am sure, delight in these exquisite drawings by Michael Partridge. No photograph could so capture the very spirit of the early days of motorcycles.

C. E. Allen BEM
Founder, The Vintage Motorcycle Club
Member, The Association of Pioneer Motorcyclists

Introduction

The earliest suggestion of a mechanically propelled cycle appears in the form of a cartoon under the impressive title 'Vélocipédraisiavaporianna'. It depicts a two-wheeled velocipede or hobby-horse, of German origin, apparently moving under the power of steam in the Luxembourg Gardens, Paris, in 1818. There is no mention as to how the contrivance actually worked, and although steam pipes appear to connect the boiler unit to points near the front and rear axles, the vital mechanism in those two areas is carefully shrouded behind clouds of steam. The vehicle probably never existed except in the imagination of some fanciful engraver who, in attempting to satirise the primitive 'Draisienne', a carriage propelled by the feet, provided an interesting and reasonably accurate prediction of the motorised cycle which emerged several decades later.

The 1820s saw steam carriages galore take to the roads of England, where they operated as a form of public transport between London and outlying districts. They were portrayed by contemporary illustrators as gargantuan, highly colourful vehicles, made of wood and iron—juggernauts of the age, with a driver on the front, fireman-engineer behind, and plenty of paying passengers sitting comfortably inside. They were not much of an improvement on horse-drawn coaches : in fact the horse was far more reliable and, owing to frequent boiler explosions and later the passing of the Red Flag Act, use and development of such vehicles was halted in England for some years. Ideas for motorised tricycles and quadri-cycles also appeared during the decade in the drawings of Shortshanks, Leech, Aitkin, and other cartoonists with whom, of course, steam locomotion was treated as a suitable subject for sarcasm, wit and humour. Artists populated the land with such nonsensical and daring vehicles as steam dragons, motorised tea-pots, horses on wheels, and gentlemen assisted by mechanical legs, all apparently leading nowhere but into a bleak future of congested roads and polluted air. But, romantic as their vehicles were, there is a possibility that some were based upon actual contraptions which the artists had seen, or perhaps more likely, had heard about. The recurring, almost identical images of small steam-powered tricycles and quadricycles, in different prints of that time, suggest that a prototype may have existed, but of this no one can be absolutely sure, not until some forty years later, in 1868, when the first known motor-cycle appeared.

It was surprisingly simple and consisted of the pedal-driven bicycle, pioneered by Ernest Michaux and introduced into England as the 'boneshaker', fitted with a tidy, compact, single-cylinder Perraux steam-engine. Drive was arranged to the rear wheel by means of pulleys and leather belts. Only one slight modification to the bicycle was required, in that the long plate spring supporting the saddle, had to be raised in order to accommodate the engine, otherwise the solid wrought-iron frame and the iron-shod, wooden wheels remained the same. A great deal of skill and nerve must have been required to ride such a machine, as stopping could only be achieved by rotating the handlebars forwards to tighten a cord and thus bring a block onto the rear tyre. Neither was it a very comfortable ride with the high wheels jarring over uneven stones and sinking into softer patches. But it did move, if only slowly and noisily, into motorcycling history, and although this vehicle was not produced in numbers, it was practical enough to provide a stimulus for other inventors. It was not long before another steam-driven boneshaker, and most likely America's first ever motorcycle, was built by Sylvester H. Roper of Roxbury.

Roper attached a twin-cylinder engine to a velocipede, one cylinder

Perhaps the first ever motorcycle, the
Vélocipédraisiavaporianna, of 1818

on each side of the frame connected by rods to driving cranks on the rear wheel axle. A firebox and boiler were suspended between the wheels, and a short chimney projected up behind the saddle. Roper modestly pronounced his creation 'a perfect triumph in mechanism' and proceeded to tour the fairs and circuses of New England, until his death in 1896, racing his steam bicycles against horses and demonstrating his steam buggies to the astonished country folk.

The penny-farthing bicycle with its huge front wheel formed the basis of Philadelphian Lucius D. Copeland's experiments during the 1880s. He installed a very elegant, lightweight steam-engine in the frame, and arranged it to drive the largest wheel by means of pulleys and a belt. The cycle could only achieve about 12mph (19.3kph) but that must have been fast enough for the driver perched on top of the large wheel, steering with the small wheel in front and controlling the steam simultaneously. It was considered safe and practical enough to merit financial backing, whereupon the inventor went one better and equipped a three-wheeler, which he called the Phaeton Moto-cycle, in similar manner. Then he found a company to market his vehicles, which were attractively arranged and capable of transporting three people at a speed of about 10mph (16.1kph) over a range of 30 miles (48.2k). Before he turned his attentions to designing motorcars, Copeland produced a steam-powered tandem which he later elaborated to include a side frame, with a wheel and seat to carry a third passenger, in a position similar to the modern sidecar. He was almost certainly the first commercial producer of motor tricycles, but his claim to have sold some two hundred models was perhaps a little exaggerated. In general, the public were not ready for personalised transport, and very few could afford such extravagances anyway. The coach and horses was still the status symbol of the rich, although it was soon to be replaced by the horseless carriages.

In England, other inventors were busy with steam tricycles. Little is known about the one a Mr Meek of Newcastle-upon-Tyne constructed for himself, other than that it was reported to be 'reliable'. A steam-driven tricycle, designed by Sir Thomas Parkyn and built by A. H. Bateman, worked well enough to attract several orders when it was exhibited at the Stanley cycle show in 1881. Their simple yet effective combination of Cheylesmore pedal tricycle and small steam-engine, might have placed England to the fore in commercial production of motor tricycles had it not been for laws, then existing, which made it practically illegal to run such vehicles on the public highway. The Locomotives on Highways Acts of 1861 and 1865, concerned with the safety of the Queen's subjects, insisted that every vehicle on the road be attended by two able-bodied men, whilst a third walked well out in front carrying a red danger flag by day, and a red lamp at night. If that was not sufficient, a speed limit of 4mph (6.4kph) was enforced in country districts, and even that was halved when passing through towns. Total emancipation from this hindrance was made statute in 1896, and until then in England—the home of mechanical enterprise—the mechanic hardly dare experiment for fear of the law and prosecution. But at the same time, France, Germany and America were already at work laying the foundation of an industry based upon the new motor carriage.

A number of steam-driven motorcycles were built after this time however, though they took the form of isolated experiments rather than production on any scale. The most notable of them was a French-built machine, later identified by the son of Heinrich Hildebrand as being a prototype for commercial production made by his father and uncle in 1889. It is thought to have been the actual

Michaux Perreaux steam motorcycle, 1869

Hildebrand steam motorcycle, 1889

machine ridden by the Frenchman Lormont in the first London to Brighton Emancipation Run of 1896. Number 51 on the official programme was a Paris steam bicycle. This machine clearly indicates the high level of development reached in steam motorcycles by the beginning of the 1890s. It utilised a Serpollet type of flash boiler carried between the wheels of a safety bicycle frame. A regular supply of small coke was delivered into the boiler from an iron hopper above, whilst water was delivered to the boiler tubes by a plunger feed pump from the 5-gallon (22.7-litre) water tank, which formed the rear mudguard. Later, Hildebrand and Wolfmuller machines were distinguished by this same feature. The rider controlled his forward speed through a wire-activated valve which regulated the quantity of water injected into the boiler. The single-cylinder, double-acting, slide-valve engine was located on the right-hand side by the rear wheel stay, and turned the rear wheel through an overhung crank, integral with the wheel hub. The front wheel was provided with a simple brake and the forks with a crude springing device. There is no record as to how this vehicle fared on the journey from London to Brighton. Some fifty-four starters, including motorised tricycles, tandems and cycles, left the Hotel Metropole at

10.30am, but owing to the unfavourable state of the roads and the foul weather, only about half of them arrived in Brighton.

There had been attempts to develop bicycles powered by energies other than steam. In 1882 a Staffordshire man, Mr Brownshill, proposed an engine that worked on air compressed into a cylinder by the motion of the bicycle wheels. The Humber Company were first in the field with an electric tandem, a practical effort intended for race track use, which attracted attention at the Stanley show in 1896 because of its neat appearance and uncomplicated design. The power plant consisted of several storage batteries linked together and connected to a motor in front of the rear wheel. It was easy to ride, and the speed was simply controlled by a single resistance placed longitudinally across the handlebars. It required no cranking, there were no troublesome carburettor settings or fuel pressures to worry about, and the vehicle was absolutely silent too. But there was a disadvantage, and one that has dogged the development of electric vehicles ever since—they can only run as long as there is charge in the battery cells, and a charge quickly runs down. However, this did not daunt the promotors of electric cab services in New York and London. The electrically powered motorcar and

Lucius D. Copelands Steam Tricycle of 1888, 'light and strong and managed easier than any horse'

local delivery vans became more popular, whilst motorcycle makers abandoned all hope of constructing a practical electric two-wheeler, although the idea was revived briefly during the 1920s.

The direct ancestor of the modern engine emerged in 1877 when Nikolaus August Otto, a German engineer, built his four-stroke internal combustion engine. The term derived from the four strokes made by the piston inside the cylinder. A means of propelling road vehicles economically was at hand, but Otto and his partner

Langen, of the Deutz gas engine works, were far too interested in making stationary engines for factory and pumping duties, etc, to bother about horseless carriages. But not so their technical director, Gottlieb Daimler (1834–1900). The pioneering Dr Otto was reluctant to accept his assistant's theory that the cumbersome, stationary gas engine, operating at 250rpm, was only a step towards a more powerful, liquid-fuel engine. After a good deal of argument, the eventual break-up came in 1882 when Daimler left the company, taking Wilhelme Maybach (who patented the float-feed carburettor in 1893) with him to Cannstatt, where they opened an experimental workshop. In the following year Daimler perfected and patented 'hot tube' ignition, although some earlier work had been carried out towards this by a man named Funk. This device employed a tube which screwed into the side of the combustion chamber and was kept hot by a bunsen burner. When the rising piston compressed the mixture in the cylinder, part of it was forced into the tube where it ignited. In 1883 Daimler produced his first compact, air-cooled, four-stroke engine, which was lighter and more powerful than previous designs. It also carried benzene as fuel in its own separate tank, and for the first time did not have to be attached by pipe to a supply of gas. Further labour and experiment resulted in a surface vaporiser, which supplied the engine with a combustible mixture of fuel and air. So far, engines had been designed with horizontal cylinders, but Daimler produced a vertical engine with fan-assisted cooling, mechanical inlet and automatic exhaust valves, internal flywheel and other advanced features. It was this engine that he installed in a crude type of boneshaker framework, and in so doing made the first recognisable suggestion of a motorcycle. It was crudely constructed of timbers with iron-shod wheels, and the single-cylinder engine, capable of an amazing 800rpm, was positioned vertically amidships, beneath the huge leather saddle in what has become a standard position. Drive to the rear wheel was via a leather belt, and braking was achieved by rotating the handlebars and dropping the belt-tension pulley through a cord. The small outrigger wheels, one on either side, were normally off the ground but could be dropped independently when necessary in order to stabilise the machine. Despite an ungainly, top-heavy appearance the vehicle did go, and during November of 1885 Daimler's son Paul, made a 3km (1.9m) run from Cannstatt to Underturkheim and back. No doubt his journey was broken more than once by the ignition burner blowing out, as they were prone to do in a wind, and which of course had to be reignited before starting off again. But what an exciting ride that must have been, and equally astonishing for the onlookers, as he bumped along the rough roads on a weird-looking mount, followed by a trail of smoke, with the unsilenced engine bellowing like mad. Not only was there danger on a path filled with ruts and holes, but also the likely risk of fire from the hot-tube ignition should the machine happen to tip over and spill fuel. The Daimlers apparently equipped this motorcycle with a spiked wheel at the rear, and an arrangement of skis at the front, and during the winter used it for joy-riding on frozen lake Cannstatt. Daimler gave no further attention to motorcycles, but the two-cylinder 'V-type' engine for which he was granted patent in 1889 was widely used by motorcar manufacturers during the following decade. Daimler can be credited with the first motorcycle and practical engine, but his idea of using two wheels instead of four was not so readily taken up by other designers. Consequently by the end of the century, the evolution of motorcycles was somewhat behind that of the motorcar, which by then had almost come to be regarded as reliable transport.

In the same year Daimler wheeled out his motorcycle, Carl Benz was

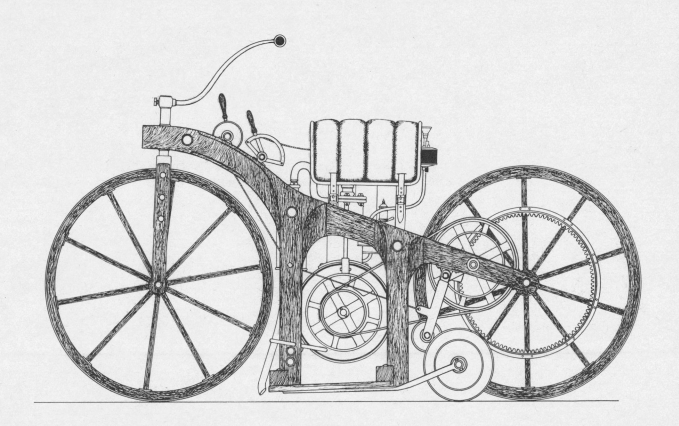

½hp Daimler motorcycle, 1885

testing a flimsy motorised tricycle. After graduating from Polytechnic School, Benz had moved about restlessly from one engineering firm to another before starting his own small workshop. He did not have a head for business matters and was bankrupt several times before 1880, when at the age of 36, with the assistance of new financial backing he founded the Mannheim Gas Engine Co, which produced small stationary gas engines to be coupled to the town's main supply. They worked successfully on a four-stroke cycle producing 250rpm, and employed a very advanced electric ignition system with battery, coil and sparking plug which Benz had devised himself. His business prospered and then, despite opposition from his associates, he became quite determined to build a car using a modified engine running on liquid fuel. The result was a spidery-looking three-wheeler which made its first public run in 1885, when it covered about 1,000m of level highway at approximately 12kph (7.5mph). It looked more like an invalid carriage than anything, but Benz was not concerned about comfort or style so much as the problems of how to keep the fuel flowing to the engine, and the engine at a steady speed without overheating. The single front wheel was for steering, and drive was transferred to the rear

wheels by belts, pulleys and side chains from a horizontal engine capable of 250–300rpm. The connecting rods and crankshaft were uncovered, as was the huge horizontal flywheel that had to be pulled around by hand in order to start the engine. Other features included the differential gear which Benz devised for the rear axle, the tubular chassis and wire spoke wheels. After the public demonstration he enlarged the engine and incorporated a low gear for hill climbing, but performance was still limited to about 12kph. However, he proved that long journeys were possible, and with the help of his family and some further financial assistance, he was able to develop his primitive design into a very elegant carriage. The first Benz motorcars were marketed in 1885 and they sold well, although the inventor tended to cling to the idea of slow, rear engines, enormous flywheels and belt drive until 1903.

In England, the first successful petrol-driven vehicle was a tricycle built by Edward Butler and displayed at the Inventors Exhibition, London in 1885. Very little is known about this quiet, withdrawn man who was born in 1863 and lived until 1940, except that he was married and had little money. A contemporary photograph shows him dressed in Sunday suit and a bowler hat, seated between the

large front wheels of his vehicle, with hands resting on the steering controls. The single, stern wheel was powered by a twin-cylinder, double-acting engine, in which the piston was driven from both ends of the cylinder by alternate explosions instead of from one end only as is usual. Steam engines were often built on the double-acting principle, but the idea was only used occasionally in petrol engines. Butler built an improved version in 1887 and called it his 'petrol-cycle'. This was also a tricycle, but the mechanical details were significantly improved. Engine power was increased from about 100–600rpm before it was successfully demonstrated to the public. Butler tried hard to interest people in his invention but he never did succeed in obtaining enough financial backing to start commercial production. Things would have no doubt been different in a country free from the restrictions which served to deter the use of mechanical road transport. In consequence, Butler's tricycle was broken up for scrap in 1896, the very year of emancipation on the roads and the inventor was sadly forgotten. A tragic end for England's first motorcycle.

¾hp Benz motor tricycle, 1885

1894 Hildebrand and Wolfmuller Motorcycle

The businesslike manufacture, and widespread distribution of motorcycles powered by internal combustion engines, can be attributed to the Hildebrand brothers of Munich, Germany. They experimented with steam power in 1889, and in 1892 tried a small two-stroke engine attached to a safety pedal bicycle. When the latter failed, they proceeded, with the assistance of Alois Wolfmuller, to install a horizontal, two-stroke, water-cooled motor in an open duplex-tube frame. The result was a very practical machine of almost modern appearance which the Hildebrand and Wolfmuller partnership produced in both France and Germany up to 1896. It had a two-cylinder engine and the pistons, which moved in unison, were connected by two parallel cranks to the rear wheel axle.

Fuel was carried in the cylindrical tank between the front down tubes of the frame, and the explosive mixture supplied to the engine by means of a surface carburettor with a mixing valve operated from the handlebars. The upper, inclined tubes held a reserve of lubricating oil for the engine, whilst the rear mudguard was also a curved water tank and carried coolant for the cylinder jackets.

The motorcycling movement had been making steady headway on the Continent before it was somewhat suddenly brought before the eyes of the British public by a colourful but rakish character named Edward J. Pennington, who came over from America in order to sell motorcycles. He immediately launched an extravagant publicity campaign and brazenly claimed his 'moto-cycle' could speed along at 65mph (104.6kph), jump across rivers and operate on paraffin because of his amazing new invention, the mysterious 'long mingling spark'. But this was all greatly exaggerated and it could do nothing of the sort. Despite Pennington's glib talk and advertising gusto, it was only a crude bicycle on small balloon tyres, with an uncooled engine and drip-feed instead of carburettor. He also presented a tandem version, but in both cases only a few models were made by the Humber Co, before they were burned out of their factory. There were also Pennington tricycles and autocars, and in spite of already having a string of disastrous projects on airships and propeller-assisted bicycles to his name, he managed to sell the British rights to a patent speculator named H. J. Lawson, for a staggering £100,000. One complete floor of Lawson's factory empire, the Great Horseless Carriage Co, was devoted solely to the construction of machines built to Pennington's design. But certain financial journals turned against the company, after which Lawson was finally ruined in 1899 by a legal action. The Humber Co revived their business and continued to produce pedal cycles, motorcycles and motor tricycles, as well as an experimental line of electric and oil tandems, but motorised tandems soon proved to be a commercial failure and were seldom used except on the racing tracks.

Hildebrand and Wolfmuller motorcycle, 1894

1896 1¾hp De Dion-Bouton Motor Tricycle

The De Dion-Bouton partnership was originally formed for the purpose of producing steam carriages, but after seeing Daimler's petrol engine at the Paris show, they were so impressed, that they set about developing an internal combustion power unit of their own. In 1895 Bouton produced a miniature engine rated at only ½hp, but when fitted behind the rear axle of an ordinary pedal tricycle, the rider

E. J. Pennington's motorcycle with 'hot-air engine'

was able to outpace pedestrians, pedal cyclists and even automobiles. The success of this vehicle even surprised the inventors and it was not long before other manufacturers saw potential in the motor tricycle. It rapidly became a popular vehicle on both sides of the Channel for competitive racing and bicycle pacing, as well as more general transport.

The illustrated De Dion-Bouton tricycle resembles an ordinary push tricycle of 1896, except that the tyres would not have had treads. A divided cylinder behind the rider's saddle

contained petrol and oil for the engine, and dry batteries were carried in the metal case attached to the top frame tube where the engine controls were also located. Fuel was supplied to the engine by a primitive surface carburettor. This was a small tank in which the volatile petrol was vaporised by the joltings of the machine, warmed by a pipe from the exhaust, and mixed with air before it was passed as a highly combustible mixture into the engine cylinder. A combined mixing and throttle valve was mounted on top of the carburettor tank, and the engine was neatly and unobtrusively fixed behind the saddle pillar, with drive taken to the rear wheel from the engine crankshaft. Pedals were included to start the engine and to assist the machine up a hard, steep climb. Some infuriated owners likened their tricycles to a treadmill because they were fitted with fixed pedalling gear, but in any form, pedals were an essential accompaniment to a temperamental engine, and it was quite reassuring to know that in the event of mechanical failure one could take off the drive belt and pedal home.

The French had already established the Paris—Bordeaux race when emancipation was achieved on the roads in Britain. Five motor tricycles—L'Hollier, a Rüb, two De Dions and a Pennington—started off in the 1896

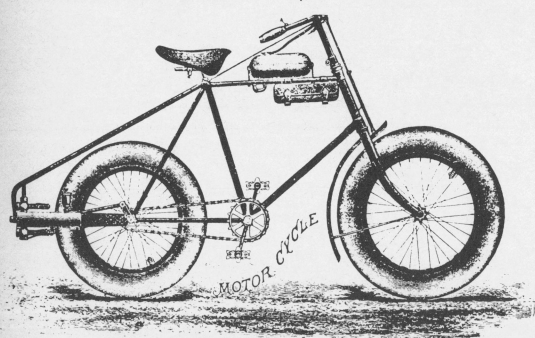

MOTOR CYCLE

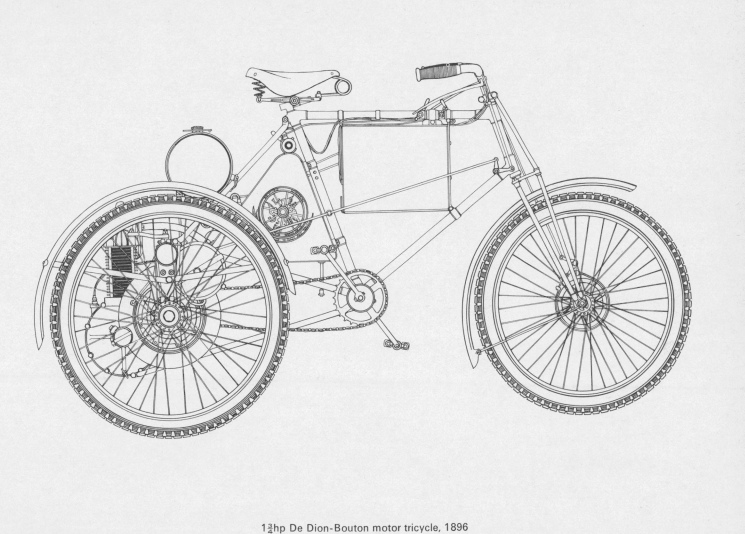

$1\frac{3}{4}$hp De Dion-Bouton motor tricycle, 1896

London to Brighton run, but only the Pennington completed the journey by nightfall. De Dions dominated racing on the Continent until Werners came along, and one of their three-wheelers maintained an average of 28mph (45.1kph) between Paris and Bordeaux in 1899. These early long-distance racers were lucky to arrive, let alone win the contest, because brakes at this time were frail and unreliable. They were pedal-cycle brakes only, with perhaps a block that pressed down onto the front tyre and a band brake at the rear. Steep hills that were, 'dangerous to cyclists' were doubly so to the motorised tricyclist and had to be descended in a laborious and steady manner, otherwise both vehicle and rider would at best end up in a ditch. Three-wheelers were very prone to tipping backwards (because the weight was behind the rear axle) and likely to overbalance sideways on bends taken at too high a speed. But on level ground, especially the long straight roads in France, the rider could lean forward over the dropped handlebars and soon outpace a fleet of pedal cyclists. As engine power was increased, so manufacturers experimented with other engine

The very stylish, French-built Leon Bollée Motor-tricycle of 1896

HURTU

DILIGEON & Cie.
Constructions

M°°N = MONNIER
8 RUE PROUDHON. BESANÇON

Ste Anme des
Voiturettes
Automobiles
Systeme LÉON BOLLÉE. Pneumatiques MICHELIN)

PARIS
MER
173 KILM
⁴⁄₁₄ ILum

ositions, particularly inside the ricycle wheelbase, in order to obtain reater stability. Experiments were lso carried out with passenger eating arrangements fastened onto he front or the rear of tricycles, and ven with two up they could still attle along at a fair rate. The first lispatch riders were mounted on 2½hp ricycles in the South African war and a imilar vehicle, the British Army's xperimental 1899 Simms Motor cout, was equipped with a Maxim un, armoured shield and 1,000 rounds f ammunition. Tricycles tended to lisappear from the roads with the dvent of 'clip-on engines'. The last le Dion three-wheeler left the actory in 1901, which was two years fter the first motorcycling fatality, vhich occurred when an Exeter man ell from his newly acquired tricycle.

eeston Motortricycle with tube ignition. 1897

The Beeston Motor Bicycle with frame built for ladies' use and detachable bar for extra strength when used by a gentleman. Fast, but not really safe due to length, weight and liability to skid on wet roads

Beeston Motor Carrier, a neat, light carrying
tricycle. The steering wheels are at the front and a
basket is placed over the rear wheel for light goods

1897 Four-cylinder Holden Motorcycle

This advanced motorcycle, almost certainly the first to have a four-cylinder engine was built in 1897 by Colonel H. C. Holden, the designer of Brooklands race track. He was a keen observer of the progress being made abroad in the development and use of petrol engines, and following the first ever motorcycle race, a 152km (94.4-miles) return run between Paris and Nantes, organised in 1896 by the Automobile Club de Paris, he was inspired to produce a motorcycle of his own design during the following year.

It was claimed to be the first all-

The popular Beeston Quadricycle of 1899

British model, and after improvements had been made to include water-jacketed cylinder barrels, it was put into commercial production for three years from 1901. The four cylinders were arranged horizontally in two parallel pairs and placed in line with the frame. The pistons of each pair were in one piece and moved together in the cylinders, being connected on each side of the machine by long rods to an overhung crank on the rear-wheel axle. This dual, direct drive from a four-cylinder engine to the road wheel, resulted in a far smoother ride than could be obtained on the belt-driven motorcycles of the time. The explosive mixture for the engine was provided by surface carburettor, secondary battery and coil-provided ignition, and the high-tension current

to four sparking plugs was distributed by a commutator on the crankshaft. Engine lubrication was provided by a simple chain pump unit, and in order to get the machine running, there was 'crypto' pedalling gear direct to the front wheel axle. The main function of this gear was to start the pistons off on their to and fro motion before the fuel ignited, but even with the engine running, pedals could be a very welcome assistance on hills. The *Cycling Magazine* maintained that no motorcycle would be a success 'that did not allow for pedalling'. Hills were a source of trouble as the angle of incline often prevented fuel flowing freely to the engine, which then petered out and allowed the machine to run backwards. Descent was always made at a snail's pace because of inefficient brakes. Holden's motorcycles gained a fine reputation for their quality of workmanship and smooth running, a feature that certainly did not apply where the final drive was by twisted rawhide belt. At best this type of belt encouraged slipping and jerking and was extremely troublesome in wet weather due to lack of grip. Composite canvas and rubber V-belts were an improvement but slipping remained a problem. Even as late as the 1920s, belt drive had advocates who were reluctant to admit that chain-drive possessed a future.

Four-cylinder Holden motorcycle, 1897

1899 ¾hp Werner Motorcycle

What may be described as the first practical motorcycle, was the brainchild of two emigré Russians, the brothers Michael and Eugene Werner, who lived in Paris. Journalists by trade, they had little technical knowledge, other than from tinkering with typewriters and phonograph mechanisms, to assist them towards developing a practical means of personal transport. But employing a process of trial and error, they first tried chain-drive to the rear wheel of an ordinary pedal bicycle from a small De Dion engine, and then obtained a more efficient arrangement the following year, 1897. This time the engine was mounted in front of the steering head, partially supported by reinforced forks, and driving the front wheel by a twisted rawhide belt. The resulting smoothness of this drive, together with a mere 65lb weight (29.5kg), went a long way towards establishing the Werner 'motorcyclette' as a practical and economical method of individual transport, although the engine was intended rather as additional power for the touring pedal cyclist, than as the sole means of bicycle propulsion.

The 1899 model illustrated, had a single-cylinder, four-stroke, air-cooled De Dion-type engine of Werner design, with 217cc capacity. The petrol tank, incorporating a wick vaporiser, was located on the frame top tube, and De Dion electric ignition system was included in preference to the original hot-tube device. Twist grip on the left handlebar controlled extra air going into the engine; the right-hand grip activated an ignition cut-out switch, whilst a handlebar lever was connected by a wire to the simple band brake on the rear wheel. Engine lubrication was supplied by a hand oilcan every 10–15 miles. The 'motorcyclette' was a sprightly machine when compared to the motor tricycles and quadricycles of the day, but unfortunately the top-heavy layout made it rather prone to side-slip on wet or greasy roads, with the additional hazard of spilt fuel catching fire. Nevertheless Werner machines enjoyed some popularity and were manufactured in England from 1898. Three years later the inventors adopted a centre-frame position for the engine, and subsequently revolutionised motor-cycling.

Early prototype motorcycles had solid tyres wired onto the wheel, the joint being effected by welding or double-threaded pipe nut. The first pneumatic tyres, invented by J. B. Dunlop in 1888, were made of canvas and rubber and had beaded edges that interlocked with an inturned wheel rim. Motorcycles were fitted with this form of tyre, but its life was short on the stony, nail-strewn roads, and they were quite likely to become detached should a sudden puncture occur. Manufacturers experimented with all manner of tyre fastenings in the form of hooks, studs, and perforations, before developing the wire suspensio variety. Other improvements included a stronger cord lining, treads all around the circumference, and satisfactory inner tubes. Tyre sections were increased from 1½in to 3in (3.8cm to 7.6cm) in order to ensure safety and comfort as motorcycles developed greater power.

A good, reliable light was a necessity, but early owners had to be content with an oil or acetylene bicycle lamp, which did not readily withstand the greater draughts and extra vibrations to which they were submitted. Lucas and other firms provided more suitable lamps after the turn of the century, but the light was still poor and tiresome to ride by for any length of time. Gas was provided by a carbide and water mixture, and illumination was increased by mirror reflectors, but it was a smelly, troublesome business and motorcyclists gratefully put these lamps to one side as dynamo lighting became available in the 1920s.

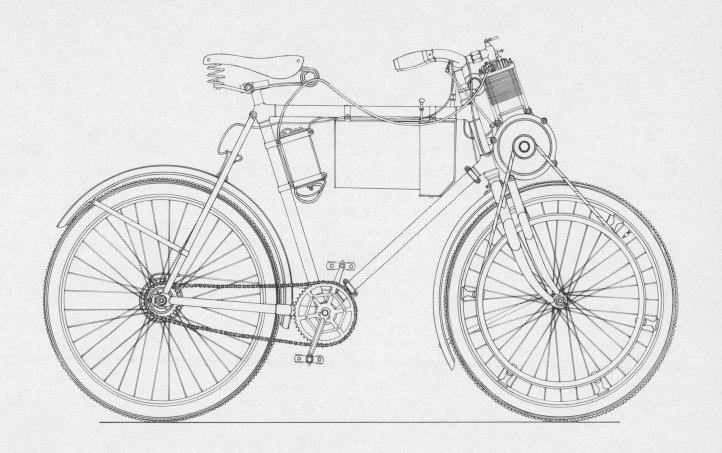

¾hp Werner motorcycle, 1899

1900 222cc Singer Motorwheel

Originally patented in 1899, by Messrs Perks and Birch of Coventry, England, the 'compact' motor-driven wheel was intended to replace the normal rear or front wheel of a pedal bicycle, or the front wheel of a pedal tricycle, and in either form it proved to be exceedingly popular. The single 222cc upright cylinder, fuel tank, surface carburettor and Simms-Bosch, low-tension magneto were contained within the aluminium-spoked wheel plates, and the whole power unit was mounted on a stationary axle to drive the wheel hub through chain reduction gear. Twist-grip throttle control was on the left-hand side of the handlebars, and mixture control located on the cross bar. There was no lubrication system, so the engine had to be

The Riley Tri-Car De-Lux. 1905

attended to manually with an oilcan every few miles. On the other hand, it averaged about 44 miles (70.8km) on 1 qt (1.1l) fuel, so quite a long journey could be completed for only a few shillings. The final 1904 version of this 26in (66cm) road wheel was spoked on one side only, giving easier access to the engine parts. Some half a century later, when severe economical pressure revived the need for cheap individual transport, similar self-contained motor wheels appeared once again in Britian and on the Continent.

By the turn of the century, Humber, Enfield, and others, had produced ladies' models, but for those females who lacked the nerve to ride solo, there was a choice of passenger position. The high wicker-work trailer, used also by pedal cyclists at the time, was beginning to decline in popularity because the increased speed of motorcycles subjected the passenger to clouds of choking dust, noxious fumes and a liberal splattering of used engine oil. Any likelihood of a lady passenger being pitched out unceremoniously and left behind in the road, should the trailer coupling break, was averted by the De Dion idea of carrying the passenger at the front of the vehicle instead of the rear. They extended the tricycle frame forward, and had two wheels instead of one with a wicker bath-chair or

bent-wood seat for the passenger between them. The other components, a single-cylinder engine, seat, handlebars and pedalling gear, stayed the same as on the tricycle, yet the vehicle had the stability of a light car. It was known as the 'quadricycle', and achieved a fair measure of popularity during the first decade, although the passenger was not protected against the weather or injury should the quadricycle run into anything.

Quadricycles could be started by pedalling, driven over all manner of appalling, hoof-battered roads without upset, and there was space for a passenger or light luggage as well. When fitted with a lady's frame, the rider was able to wear a warm top-coat or mackintosh in wet weather, while the central position left him well clear of wheel spray. The Progress, Riley, Beeston, Ariel and Dennis Companies produced quadricyles on De Dion lines, but they tended to disappear from the roads as 'clip-on' engines became available for motorcycles.

222cc Singer motorwheel, 1900

1901 2½hp Clyde Motorcycle

Mr Waite of Leicester, England, had used the loop frame for his Clyde motor bicycles a year or so before it was featured by other makers such as Quadrant, James, and Clarendon. A Leicestershire doctor originally purchased this machine for about 55 guineas (£57.75) and used it to cover his daily rounds for many years. The 302cc engine was served by a Longuemare carburettor and Simms-Bosch, low-tension magneto. The fuel tank contained 1 gal petrol (4.5l), enough for about 70 miles (approximately 113km) of running, whilst one pint of lubricating oil was gradually delivered to the engine by a hand operated pump. The wheels had hollow section rims, which generally went out about 1900, and were fitted with 28in by 2in (71.7cm by 5cm) beaded-edge tyres. The rear wheel incorporated a Chater-Lea, back-pedalling brake, and a spoon brake, operated by handlebar lever, worked on the front wheel tyre. Clyde Motorcycles continued up to about 1914, after which the firm concentrated on motorcar production.

Pedalling gear in the early years was standard push bicycle type, and not really capable of withstanding the frequently desperate effort required to start an engine. The gear often seized up or became fixed in both directions, going round and round at high speed rapping the rider's ankles, until the engine was stalled, or perhaps the pedals suddenly became free with even more painful consequences, especially if the rider were taking the strain off the engine on a hill. Back-pedalling brakes often locked the wheel and had to be used with extreme caution on wet or greasy roads. Riders were recommended to apply the front brake before the rear wheel brake, followed by increasing pressure on both controls, otherwise one wheel would probably lock momentarily and result in an uncontrollable skid. Quite a number of new lightweight motorcycles, many of them powered by Minerva engines came onto the market in 1901, and the number of models on display at the Stanley show increased to over a hundred. There had been eight in the 1898 show.

Pedal cyclists had been agitating for better roads since the mid 1880s, but they were still not much improved. In the towns and cities, a novice rider had to negotiate a network of cobbled streets and tramlines that became slippery and dangerous with rain. Riding along in the wake of a tram or motorcar was also a risky business, as neither were in the habit of giving a warning when about to pull up. Motorcycling in the country was a precarious adventure too, as the roads were full of holes, and little better than cart tracks. Certain skills and a lot of wristwork were required in dodging stray sheep, stones and swampy patches, whilst the rutted surface and lack of frame springing hammered the rider's bones until they ached. Long journeys were not readily undertaken because of the likelihood of mechanical failures, and whilst minor breakdowns could be put right on the roadside, anything more serious meant hiring a cart in order to get home. It was quite easy to outpace bicycle riders who wished to engage in an unofficial race along the way, but at times the motorcyclist could be brought to a sudden and unexpected halt by the appearance of a horse, which, according to an order of 1904 'had the right of way over a motor vehicle'.

Weather protection hardly existed or motorcycles yet, so it was necessary to dress up in a long leather coat or trenchcoat, cap, gauntlets and leggings in order to avoid being saturated or frozen, but nothing it seems could dampen a growing enthusiasm for the open road and the sport attached to motorcycling.

2½hp Clyde motorcycle, 1901

1902 2hp Werner Motorcycle

The Werner brothers were first to produce a motorcycle in which the pedal bracket of the frame was replaced by a vertical engine. They revised their top-heavy 'motorcyclette' design completely in 1901, and the new engine position, low in the frame, midway between front and rear wheel, was outstandingly successful when compared with other arrangements of the day. The new Werner model displayed qualities of road-holding and controllability far superior to any other two-wheeler then on the road. The bicycle frame remained much the same as before, except the pedals were removed further back into an auxiliary position in order to accommodate the engine, and an extra, frame-strengthening member was installed below the fuel tank. Other new features included engine controls mounted on the handlebars, a spray-carburettor instead of the primitive surface vaporiser type, plus hand-pump lubrication (which required a few strokes of the plunger every few miles), rather than the unreliable drip feed system. Getting the machine to go was the all important thing during those early days, but bringing it safely to a halt seems to have been an afterthought in most cases. This model had only a crude brake operating onto the front tyre, and a foot-operated lever that forced a fibre block unit into a channel on the belt rim of the rear wheel, slowing it down and eventually causing it to stop.

Werner sales were given an international boost when one of their new models won the 1902 Paris to Vienna Race with the French rider Bucquet in the saddle, a victory which not only marked the beginnings of the company's racing achievements, but also the general acceptance of this new-style motorcycle. Incidentally, the captain of the newly-formed MCC (Motor Cycling Club) led the club's first run to Brighton during 1902 on a Werner machine. The company opened a branch factory at Coventry, producing $2\frac{3}{4}$hp and $3\frac{1}{4}$hp engines, but the vertical twin which they also produced, failed to catch on because of mechanical complications and excessive vibration.

Meanwhile motorcycle sport was growing in popularity. Many cycle tracks on the outskirts of cities in England and France began to feature motorcycle events as well as pedal cycle races, whilst the local constabulary very kindly turned a blind eye to reliability trials and sprint events held on deserted stretches of public highway in their district. Bicycle clubs began to form motor-cycling sections, as more of their members realised the advantages of a powered two-wheeler. Cycle tracks in Britain were unsuitable for high-speed motorcycle racing but speeds in the region of 70mph (approximately 113kph) were possible on the steeply-banked velodromes in France. This encouraged riders to build colossal motorcycles and tricycles powered by massive engines of more than 2,000cc, which were far too heavy and out of all proportion to the strength of frame and wheels. The Autocycle Club, formed in 1903 for the advancement of autocycling, turned its back on this freakish form of racing and set about the task of inaugurating a contest for road-going machines. There was little hope of ever obtaining official permission from Westminster to race on public roads in England, so the club approached the Tynwald Government on the Isle of Man which quickly passed an Act, closing 16 miles (25.8km) of road for TT (Tourist Trophy) competitions.

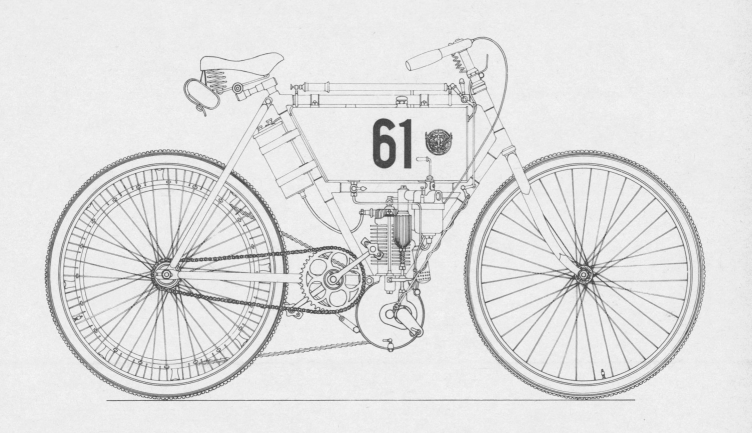

2hp Werner motorcycle, 1902

1902   2¾hp Excelsior Motorcycle

During the early years of the century there was little, if any, uniformity amongst makers as to where the engine should be attached to the bicycle. Some followed the Werner brothers' split frame design, whilst others employed a loop frame, or a cradle between the front down tube and bottom bracket. Some manufacturers preferred a frame with the engine mounted between double front down tubes, and Joah Phelon almost completely replaced the down tube with a forward-inclined engine. Those who favoured the powerful big De Dion engine, made under licence by the Motor Manufacturing Co, Coventry, found that it could not be installed below the front down tube of a diamond-style bicycle frame until the frame had been redesigned. Bayliss, Thomas and Co, were one of the manufacturers who adopted this change on their 'Excelsior' motorcycle. An almost identical model to the one shown here, took the world speed record at the Canning Town cycle track, London, in 1902, with Harry Martin in the saddle. Amazingly, it covered 1 mile (1.6km) in 1min 24secs from a standing start.

The illustrated machine was originally purchased by Caleb Wilson of Durham, England, on 28 June 1902, for 45 guineas (£47.25) and the 411cc engine is still capable of 50mph (80.5kph). It had a surface carburettor, De Dion high-tension ignition, mechanical exhaust and automatic inlet valve.

Nickel plating on brass was generally used for fittings, and time was still spent in neatly finishing the frame and mudguards with black enamel and gold-leaf lining. There was direct belt drive to the rear wheel and no clutch, so pedals were used for starting the engine. A German newspaper of the day deplored the general lack of ladies' models, 'for our sporting comrades of the fair sex are showing great interest in the little *teuf-teuf*'. Showing interest was one thing, but starting the beastly thing was another, and many a capable fellow was reduced to the depths of despair in this endeavour. Coaxing an engine to start from cold was more or less impossible in the early days until some fast pedalling had been done with the rear wheel up on a stand. Rotating the engine in this way helped break down the glutinous engine oil, and rocking the machine encouraged the petrol to vaporise. New owners often failed to start their engines for several days and usually half killed themselves, running and pedalling along the street until they were exhausted or the engine fired—only to die away again after a few yards. Leather gaiters were a must for all pioneer riders, not so much to protect their trousers, but to guard the shins and calves against gashes shoul a boot suddenly slip off the whirling pedals. Lucky owners lived at the top of a hill which was usually enough to get them started from cold, but it was no joke pushing a machine of tolerable weight back to the top if it refused. Improved ignition and carburation made starting somewhat easier, but even so, running and jumping on remained a frightening necessity until kick-starters were incorporated.

2¾hp Excelsior motorcycle, 1902

1903 2¾hp Quadrant Motorcycle

Quadrant of Birmingham, England, under the direction of W. Lloyd, contributed a great deal towards the development and manufacture of ordinary pedal bicycles before appearing amongst pioneers of the English motorcycle industry. Their first machine, the Quadrant Forecar, was powered by a 211cc Minerva engine, but by 1903, in common with some other English manufacturers, they succeeded in becoming independent of continental manufacturers and installed their own engines. The neatly designed 2¾hp Quadrant was amongst top sellers in the new motorcycle boom, and could be purchased for 42 guineas (£44.10). The compact engine was sloped forward on a loop frame and the various control levers which normally adorned the top tube were combined into the single lever located on the right-hand side of the petrol tank. It had a cubic capacity of 375cc, automatic inlet valve, side-valve exhaust and surface carburettor, and the ignition was by trembler coil. Final drive was a belt to the rear wheel with pedal and chain assistance, and at some time, a free engine clutch was included on the engine drive pulley.

The well-designed and superbly finished JAP engines were introduced in 1903. During the same year the merits of lightweight motorcycles were advanced to the public, and prospective purchasers of pedal cycles were asked to consider a 1½hp or 1¾hp motorcycle instead. By this time the only bicycle makers of note who had not marketed a motorcycle were Rover, and Rudge Whitworth, and they were expected to conform soon. Ladies and elderly gentlemen were beginning to take an interest in motorcycling, and called for a vibrationless machine that was easy to start, had two gears and an average speed of about 20mph (35kph). Motorcycling was beginning to catch on both as a pastime and a sport—one enthusiast of the day 'bought a machine; had 15 minutes tuition in Hyde Park, then covered 258 miles in 3 days', until his progress was halted by piston seizure through having forgotten to pump oil into the engine.

People naturally wanted to race their newly acquired machines, and a class for motorcycles was included in many of the old town-to-town motorcar races. A rider in the Paris to Madrid 1903 road race, claimed to have maintained an average of 38mph (61 kph), in spite of dogs and cattle wandering all over the roads. In the Glasgow to London non-stop trial that same year, all nine entrants reached London safely, the only machine to make an involuntary stop being Tom Silver's Quadrant. Motorcycle police were not yet favoured by the authorities, because it was thought their travelling at speed in pursuit of other vehicles would only constitute another danger on the road but some instruction was taken by the police on the use and management of motorcycles with regard to escorting VIPs.

$2\frac{3}{4}$hp Quadrant motorcycle, 1903

1903 3hp Harley Davidson Motorcycle

One of the greatest names in American motorcycle production was and still is Harley Davidson, founded in 1903 by two amateur inventors, William Harley and Arthur Davidson. They produced their first motorcycle in a small backyard workshop, and went from strength to strength until by mid-century they were the only major motorcycle manufacturers in the USA. Their original intention was to take the effort out of bicycling, and they were assisted in this spare-time task by another Davidson brother, who was an expert toolmaker, and a German draughtsman who knew something about De Dion engines. Since nothing was available in the way of engine parts, everything had to be made by hand, the carburettor for example, was fashioned out of an old tomato can. It took them many months of spare-time work to reach the trial stage, but all that time they were convinced the machine would work. Onlookers, however, were amazed when at last the engine started and Harley rode the motor-cycle slowly round the yard. It did not move very fast, but it did go. The 2hp engine was found to be just about powerful enough for level roads, but

in need of some leg assistance on hills. Even more determined to take the effort out of bicycling Harley and Davidson returned to work and increased the engine capacity from 410cc to 475cc, and in order to obtain smoother running, they increased the 5in (12.7cm) diameter flywheel to more than double its original size. Drive to the rear wheel was by means of a flat belt via a large pulley attached to the wheel rim, and as there was only one gear and no clutch, the rider had to run and push, then pedal away to get the engine started and the motorcycle in motion. The loop frame, adopted very early by Harley Davidson, added to the true motorcycle appearance of their first model, as compared with their contemporaries, who used diamond-style bicycle frames with engines bolted on. Soon more workshop space was required, so a larger wooden hut was built and 'The Harley Davidson Motorcycle Co.' was painted over the door.

Thus it was in 1903 that the first factory was in operation, and the first three Harley Davidson motorcycles to come off the production line were actually sold before they were made. From then on the firm expanded to produce 5 motorcycles in 1906, and 150 motorcycles in 1907, during which year the company secured incorporation and issued their first

advertising brochure. In 1909 the first Harley Davidson 6hp V-twin was introduced, and during 1917–18, factory production was devoted exclusively to military motorcycles, of which 20,000 were made. American speed cops were invariably mounted on powerful Harley Davidson and Indian machines, which contributed to the success of both firms.

The year 1908 marked the entrance of Harley Davidson into the field of sporting competition and the period 1914–18 saw their special racing motorcycles score overwhelming victories in long-distance and cross-country events. Dirt-track racing was becoming established on the hot, dusty, horse tracks in America, but neither these circuits nor the wooden board tracks were large enough to contain the powerful V-twins which could lap at over 70mph (113kph) and so motorcycle races shared the automobile tracks at Indiana, Marion and Illinois, etc. High speeds began to make headlines in America during 1902, when Albert Champion covered 1 mile (1.6km) of a circular track in 1min 10sec, and Oscar Hedstrom, designer of the original Indian motorcycle rode a 1min 3sec mile on Florida beach. The Federation of American Motorcyclists was formed in the same year for the purpose of furthering motorcycle sport, and racing developed on a large scale.

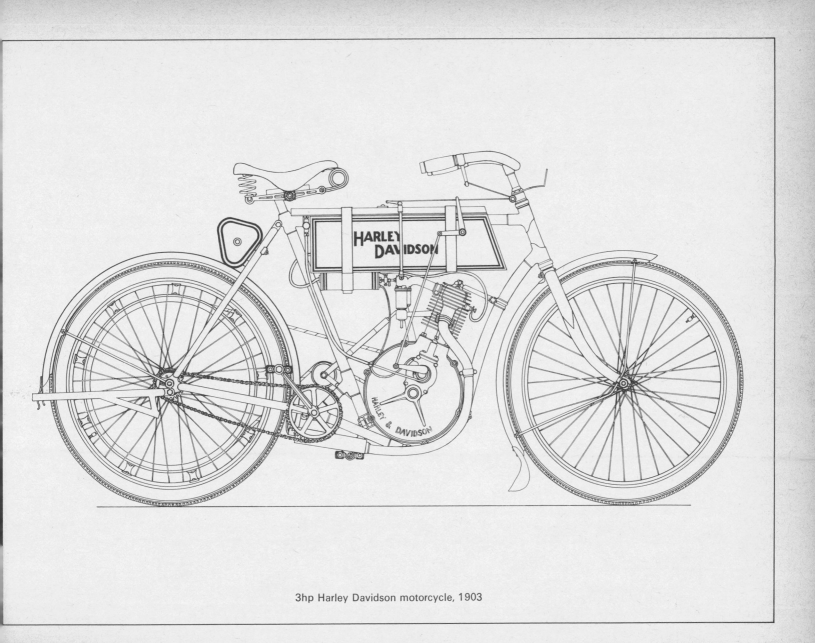

3hp Harley Davidson motorcycle, 1903

1904 3½hp Phelon & Moore Forecar

This vehicle was probably one of a small number manufactured by the Humber Co of Coventry, under licence from P & M Motorcycles, Cleckheaton in Yorkshire. The 372cc P & M engine with Vapp carburettor and accumulator ignition, was inclined forwards and built into the frame with drive to the rear wheel via chains and the P & M two-speed gear designed by Mr Moore in 1904. Three years earlier, Joah Phelon had patented this new style of frame with the engine in place of the front down tube, and he received a 7s 6d (37½p) royalty on each one made by Humber. The four long rods which held cylinder head and crank case together, were extended from the bottom lug to the head lug in order to form a frame member, and remained a distinguishing feature of P & M motorcycles. The motorcycle, forecar attachment provided a pleasant and comfortable vantage point for a lady passenger, but however comfortable, it was not always safe, since excessive vibration due to the unmade roads of the time, often caused the couplings to loosen and the forecar to swerve out of line alarmingly or even turn over. J. Van Hooydonk pioneered forecar design in 1902 when he built a light forecarriage to replace the front wheel of his Phoenix motorcycle, and so converted it into a two-seater tricycle. The idea had been tried out earlier, but Hooydonk attracted attention to his design by winning a gold medal in the 1,000-mile (1,609km) Autocycle Club's reliability trial. He marketed his forecar as the Phoenix Trimo and provided it with fittings for attachment to any make of motorcycle. Conversion back to solo took only a few minutes whenever the lady decided to stay at home.

The Trimo was soon copied by other makers. Humber, Excelsior and Mills & Fulford were amongst those who wheeled out almost identical designs with open wicker seats, before the trend of 1904 changed towards coach-built seating with sprung supports—which in effect made the whole arrangement less stable and more prone to vibration on rough roads. Overheating was common, because a forecar tended to block the flow of air to the engine, and experiments were carried out with ducted air and multiple radiators in order to remedy it. As engine power was increased, the bicycle's frame and wheels had to be strengthened considerably in order to contain the greater power, but at this point the vehicle diverted away from motorcycle development and instead became a tricar. Speed and hill-climbing performance were improved with 6hp and 9hp engines, but vibration remained troublesome despite additional leaf springing on the rear wheel.

With upholstered bucket seats, steering wheel, instrument board and suggestion of enveloping bodywork, the non-convertible tricar was a very short-lived rival to the light motorcar. They cost about the same, but tricar performance was not as good. Motorists were not very interested in them and production had almost ceased by 1910, by which time motorcycle passenger travel had been made much safer with the advent of the sidecar outfit. First patented in 1903 by W. G. Graham, and put onto the market in the same year by Mills & Fulford, it soon eclipsed the forecar and other passenger positions, with the exception of the pillion.

3½hp P & M Forecar, 1904

1905   2½hp Joseph Barter Motorcycle

In 1905 a Bristol man, J. F. Barter, produced an unusual, horizontal, twin-cylinder cycle motor for attachment to an ordinary pedal bicycle frame. Originally known as the Fee, then as the Fairy, it was the first horizontally opposed, twin-cylinder unit to be produced in quantity, and was destined to form a basis for the later and well-known line of Douglas motorcycles. Barter's original engine was a 2½hp twin-cylinder, air-cooled unit clipped onto the tubes of a pedal cycle frame. Drive was by a primary chain to a small countershaft gear-box on the front down tube and thence by rawhide belt to the rear wheel. The outfit was lightweight and economic, and provided the means for a pleasant ride out at speeds up to 20mph (32 kph). Douglas Brothers were a firm of Bristol engineers making machinery for the boot and shoe trade, when W. W. Douglas took over the rights of manufacture from Barter's Light Motors Co. The first 2¾hp Douglas motorcycle appeared in 1907. It had direct belt drive, but retained the diamond-shape, pedal-cycle-type frame of Barter's Fairy, until the characteristic Douglas-style frame, with sprung forks, was designed in the following year.

Some attempt was now being made to place Britain on a higher level in international motorcycle racing. Prior to the first TT race in 1907, a group of riders entered for an annual event called the International Road Race, but the British had not taken the trouble to prepare, and left the field wide open for the French in 1904, and the Austrians in 1905. In order to strengthen the team, some eliminating trials were held on the Isle of Man, and again at Knowlsey Park, England, in 1906, but only five people entered. When the 1906 final was run, the Austrian riders were again first and second, with Harry Collier's Matchless coming along half an hour later in third place. There was a good deal of discontent amongst the competitors afterwards, concerning the organisation of the race and Austrian team's tactics in particular, so the series was cancelled.

The Mills and Fulford sidecar, with basketwork body and trailing wheel

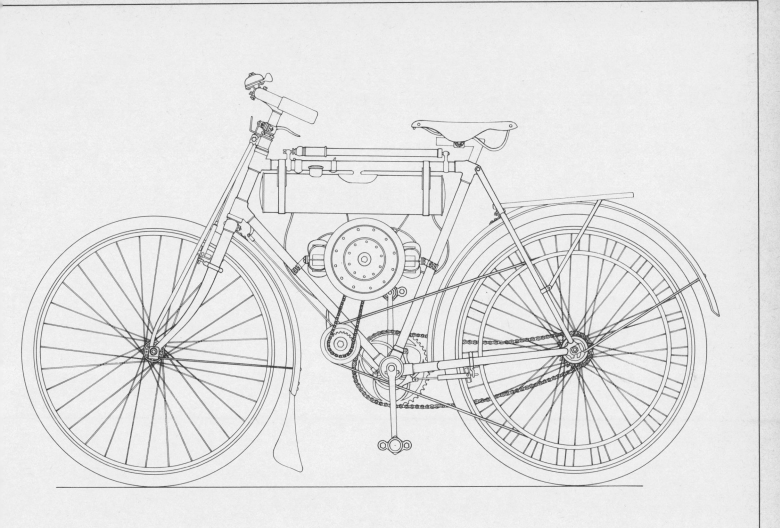

2½hp Joseph Barter motorcycle, 1905

1907 3hp Triumph Motorcycle

During the early years, Triumph Pedal Cycle Co was directed by Siegfried Bettman and a young German named Maurice Schulte, who in 1885 had gone to Coventry to exhibit the Hildebrand and Wolfmuller motorcycle. Triumph begain to build lightweight motorcycles with JAP engines in 1903, and soon followed these with larger models powered by Fafnir units. By 1906 they were using their own 3hp single-cylinder engines in a model which, besides being essentially very simple in design, included such advanced items as spray carburettor, high-tension magneto, ball-bearings on the engine mainshaft, and pivot-springing of the front forks. The fine reputation gained by Triumph for their quality of finish and mechanical reliability, was reflected by increased sales at the very time when motorcycle registrations were beginning to fall. The factory produced and sold more than 1,000 motorcycles during 1907, and in 1908 alone, made a profit of £22,084—a figure which more than doubled in the following year, when over 3,000 Triumph motorcycles were purchased and put onto the road. On the Isle of Man, in 1907, the first ever TT race for single-cylinders was won by

Collier's Matchless, with Triumph Riders Marshall and Hulbert occupying second and third places. High speeds were not a feature of the first TT race, and fuel economy was enforced quite rigorously—the single-cylinder machines were allowed 1gal (4.5l) for 90 miles (114.8km), and the twins, 1gal (4.5l) for 75 miles (120.7km). Pedalling was freely employed on all the upgrades.

Triumph increased power for the following year and produced an engine which not only proved extremely suitable for touring outfits, but also very efficient for racing as it powered Jack Marshall to first place in the 1908 TT. He covered the $158\frac{1}{8}$-mile (254.5-km) course at an average speed of 40.49mph (65.16kph).

By the outbreak of World War 1, Triumph had increased their single-cylinder engine capacity to 4hp in order to make it suitable for sidecar outfits as well as for solos. They also produced a successful 650cc, vertical, twin-cylinder unit, the forerunner of much modern engine design, and a type which Triumph revived during the mid 1930s. The company produced a large number of motorcycles for the Allies during World War I, especially the new model H, a 550cc single-cylinder SV design with chain-cum-belt drive from a three-speed countershaft gear-box—a model much favoured by Army dispatch riders. The

1920s saw co-operation between Triumph and the fuel technologist, Harry Ricardo, who, having designe very successful OHV engine conversion for the firm's 500cc racin machines, adapted it to the ordinary road-going motorcycle, known from then as the Triumph Ricardo—a very successful, high-speed model that enjoyed wide sales. Triumph's greatest technical success came afte 1935, when Edward Turner designed the 500cc, vertical 'speed-twin'. It had a compact, quiet-running engine with outstanding qualities of acceleration and speed, which established a really high standard for all modern vertical-twin design.

3hp Triumph motorcycle, 1907

1907 944cc NLG Peugeot Motorcycle

The new Brooklands motor racing track was opened in 1907, but motorcycle racing was not held there until the following season. The first actual race to be arranged for two-wheelers on the Brookland circuit took place in February 1908, when a private match between O. L. Bickford's Vindec and W. C. McMinnies' TT Triumph, resulted in a win for the latter. The spectacle proved to be so thrilling, that a full scale motorcycle race was arranged to take place in the following April at the Easter Monday car meeting, an event which attracted twenty-four riders mounted on machines between 330cc and 1000cc. The powerful, single-speed, belt-drive NLG Peugeot, ridden by W. E. Cook, proved to be superior on the day and finished about half a mile ahead of its rivals, having covered the 5½ miles (8.9km) of the race at an average speed of 63mph (101.4kph). Cook achieved the better average of 70mph (112.7kph) on his NLG in the following year, and this combination of man and machine remained supreme for some time afterwards.

His NLG model, produced by North London Garages, was powered by a 944cc V-twin Peugeot engine. It was built purely for speed and all rider comfort was sacrificed in order to achieve as light a weight as possible. The frame was sparse, wheels were spoked with thin wires, front forks rigid and supported by flimsy stays, the saddle was taken from a bicycle and the handlebars swept low even for a racing motorcycle. There was no clutch provided so the engine was started in customary Brooklands manner, by running down the test hill. As a means of further reducing the overall weight, several cooling fins were filed away from the cylinder and a good deal of drilling carried out on the engine plates, nuts, clips, and control levers, until the whole assembly weighed only 118lb (53.5kg). This was common practice amongst racers. There was no easy way of winning a speed event, and knocking off fractions of a second involved countless hours of arduous preparation—thinning down engine parts and burnishing all moving parts to reduce friction, before finally reassembling the engine with extreme care. Hotting-up required plenty of money as well as time, and here the lone hand was often at a disadvantage. Special items had to be purchased, such as ribbed tyres and racing fuels, while frequent and thorough maintenance was necessary in order to retain a high state of mechanical efficiency. These lean, sleek racing machines could not be used away from the track for fear of upsetting the fine state of tuning, and had to be pushed and carried from one venue to another on the running boards of a motorcar.

Sheer riding ability played as important a part as anything in speed competitions, and even with a machine in full trim, a rider still had to have some tricks up his sleeve. Brooklands was almost a 3-mile (4.8-km) circuit, and the surface quite bumpy, so racing men had to gain a thorough knowledge of all the ripples and dips before they were able to steer an instinctive course combining both safety and speed. The strength and direction of wind were important too, especially when scorching along only inches away from the edge of the track, and shelter provided by the aviation sheds, trees, shrubs, and even grasses all played a part when striving to increase lap speeds by points of a second. In 1909 the makers of NLG achieved further acclaim when another of their machines, powered by a 2,913cc V-twin JAP engine, reached 90mph (144.8kph), but by then, in the regular motorcycle racing held at Brooklands, the more powerful machines were handicapped in order to provide more equal competition and exciting finishes.

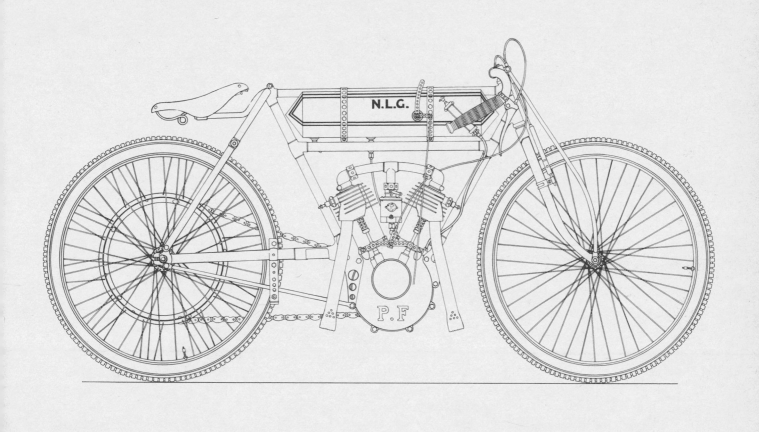

944cc NLG Peugeot motorcycle, 1907

1910 Vindec Special Motorcycle

There was no commercial, technical or other association between Vindec motorcycles made by Brown Bros, of London, and the Vindec Specials built in Germany by the Allright (Tiger) factory. The latter were imported into Britain by the South British Trading Co, between 1903 and 1914, and utilised a number of proprietary engines, including FN, JAP, Minerva, Fafnir and Peugeot.

The years following 1910 saw the development of an odd little vehicle called the cycle car. This was built from the basic components of the motorcycle—a single, twin-cylinder or air-cooled, four-in-line engine mounted on a wood and metal chassis, with belt or chain transmission and three or four wheels. Ideal perhaps for the lad whose parents would not let him own a motorcycle on the grounds that two-wheelers were dangerous. Cycle cars were fast, sporty and considerably cheaper than contemporary light cars, but the design was generally doubtful and they vibrated like mechanical jellies. Dubious braking, side-by-side or tandem seating, cable and bobbin steerage, controls on the outside, and a flimsy plywood or light metal body completed the assembly, which was left totally devoid of any weather protection. Some later models were provided with hoods, glass wind-screens, full bonnets, and mudguards, but they were not built in the true spirit of motorcycles, and came nearer the category of light motorcars.

There were some sixty makes of cycle car on the market by 1912, and they remained popular as runabouts for quite a few years, reappearing again after the Armistice. Most successful amongst the four-wheelers were the English-built Rollo and the French 8hp Bedelia, a risky contraption that was steered from the back seat with the passenger sitting in front. Morgans were the notable three-wheelers, with V-twin engine mounted on the nose, and chain drive to the rear wheel. Many motorcycle firms in Britain made tentative moves towards the car industry with a small four-wheeler about this time, and additional models, the Imp and the Woods Mobilette came from America. The two-wheeler car made spasmodic appearances up to 1926, but despite the efforts of such designers as A. V. Roe, the pioneer airman, who used one as his personal runabout, they failed to impress the public. The French Monotrac, with tandem seats, high-sided body with enveloping wind-shield and hood, was a very practical effort and a similar vehicle was made by Ner-a-Car in England. Someone suggested that it might be a good idea to market a cheap four-wheeler chassis, so that when winter set in the motorcyclist could remove the engine from the frame and install it in the chassis, but this was just another idea that failed to catch on. Cycle cars declined when mass production of baby motorcars started in the 1920

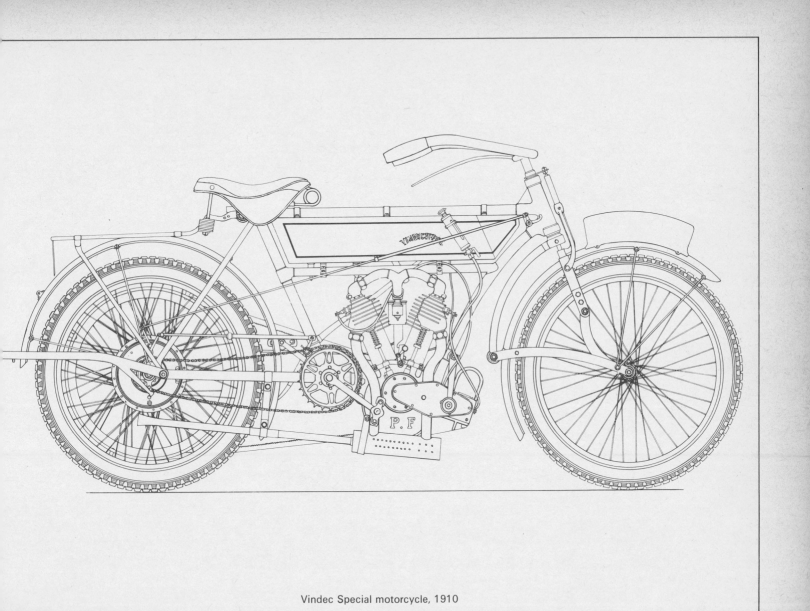

Vindec Special motorcycle, 1910

1912 500cc FN Motorcycle

A number of manufacturers began to install compact, smooth-running, four-cylinder, air-cooled engines during the latter part of 1904. Most notable of the designs were the Belgian FN, German Dürkopp, Austrian Laurin and Klement, and the British Binks. The very successful FN, a product of the arms factory Fabrique Nationale d'Armes de Guerre, of Liege, Belgium, employed a 3hp, four-in-line engine with enclosed shaft and bevel gear drive to the rear wheel. It was built to the design of Paul Kelecom, and launched amid the publicity surrounding a road tour of Europe, the finish of which coincided with the opening of the Paris Salon in late 1904. FN produced motorcycles in this form, but with different capacities, until 1923, at which point the famous FN 4 was followed by a very orthodox-looking 350cc, side-valve single, and then a chain-driven, 'monobloc', 500cc, overhead-valve single. The company participated for many years in road racing as well as at Brooklands and the Isle of Man, and their factory supplied Army motorcycles during two wars.

There were a greater number of motorcycles on the roads in France during the early years of the century than in Britain, but the balance had altered by about 1910. However, popularity revived again following World War I, and French models continued their tendency to be smaller and lighter than the British counterpart. In addition they usually lacked such refinements as kick-starters, clutches and variable gears for reasons of economy, as French motorcyclists generally showed little concern for mechanical excellence, and simply required cheap and reliable transport.

The motorcycle industry in Germany underwent a rapid revival during the early 1920s, despite this country's difficult economic situation after the war. The Ardic and DKW factories did pioneering work with two-strokes, and in addition to the conventional models on the market, there were also some highly speculative designs such as the Megola, with a five-cylinder, radial engine housed inside the front wheel. Great interest was aroused in 1923 when the BMW aero-engine works produced the first of their famous 500cc transverse-twins, with shaft drive and a powerful unit-constructed engine which emitted only a quiet hum even at high speed. The design echoed Granville Bradshaw's earlier ABC flat-twin for the Sopwith Aviation Co.

There was a revival of interest in other continental countries during the early 1920s, but motorcycle transport was not encouraged by the very poor state of the roads, and apart from the sporting fraternity, the main users were artisans and workmen who required an economical form of vehicle to get to and from work. Cycle motor units were popular on the Continent long before economic pressure required their use in Britain. They usually clipped onto the steering head and drove the front wheel by means of a friction roller or chain, or alternatively, powered the rear cycle wheel in much the same manner.

500cc FN motorcycle, 1912

1912 2¾hp Douglas Model K Motorcycle

The model K was the de luxe model in the range being equipped with such refinements as two-speed gearbox, free engine clutch, footboards and kick-starter. The latter item is unfortunately missing from the machine illustrated here, as is the original Douglas carburettor which at some time was replaced by a superior AMAC unit. The 348cc, horizontally-opposed, twin-cylinder engine with its large external flywheel and Bosch magneto, was located in the frame above the lower horizontal tube in characteristic Douglas style. Transmission to the rear wheel was by chain cum belt through a two-speed, $5\frac{1}{2}$:1 and $8\frac{1}{2}$:1 ratio, Douglas gear-box and cone clutch. This well-balanced machine achieved considerable popularity because of its easy starting and handling qualities, and could originally be purchased for £50.

The company went on to produce 2¾hp solo motorcycles for the British forces during World War I, as well as flat-twin, 500cc and 600cc models. The leather pouch strapped to the rear carrier, or perhaps mounted on the tank top, contained sufficient tools to deal with simple roadside repairs. Manufacturers provided a basic tool kit and tyre pump with every machine purchased, but the 'old hands' tucked in all sorts of oddments, such as chewing gum to plug a leaking petrol tank, a flash-lamp to aid repairs in the dark, a small can of oil to deal with seized-up parts, a nearly new spark plug, and a spare valve, whilst odd lengths of wire and various nuts and bolts added to the feeling of security. As there were very few garages along the road in those days, the enthusiast had not only to be ready for his own eventualities but those of fellow riders as well. Standardisation of parts was much better by now, and any rider forced to ditch his machine overnight, because of serious breakdown or a puncture, could almost guarantee that the part he took back next day would fit. The AA (Automobile Association) began to gain a lot of support from motorcyclists, not only because it offered such practical assistance as kerbside repairs and touring facilities, but because motorcycling organisations believed they had to unite in some way as a measure of resistance against increasingly hostile public opinion.

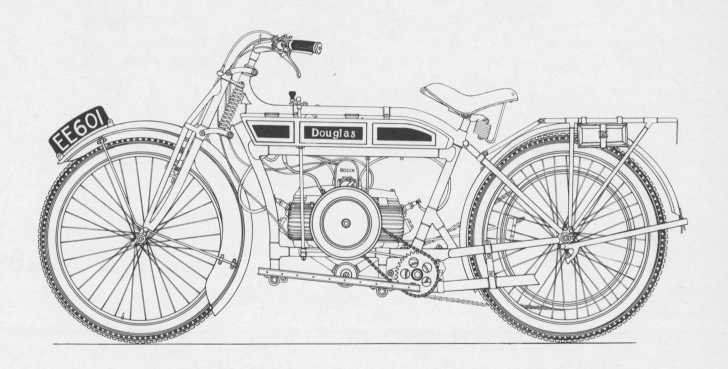

$2\frac{3}{4}$hp Douglas model K motorcycle, 1912

1912 3hp Pearson-Cox Steam Bicycle

The Pearson Cox Steam Co started operations at Shortlands in Kent during 1910. They were mainly concerned with the production of compact steam cars, but development was hampered by financial difficulties, and the company's closure was enforced after only seven years. During that time they showed some interest in steam as a motive power for two-wheeler vehicles, having produced and sold a number of rather orthodox-looking steam bicycles in 1912. The simple, yet effective, arrangement of parts was similar to that of the Serpollet steam car, but was simplified by the elimination of condenser and much of the automatic mechanism. A single-cylinder, single-acting engine was mounted on the seat-post between the rear wheel and the large triangular tank containing lubricating oil and sufficient water for 40 miles (64km), whilst the cylindrical tank over the rear mudguard contained paraffin for heating the semi-flash generator, located on the frame behind the front wheel. The supply of water to it was controlled by two valves operated separately from handlebar levers through Bowden wires, and the varying supply of water controlled the machine's forward speed. The engine could be set for any desired speed by a ratchet on the left handlebar, whilst the right handlebar control was used to by-pass the feed water completely, whenever it was necessary to make an emergency stop. A hand pump on the right side of the tank supplied oil for the splash lubrication system, and required one stroke every 9 miles (14.5km). The various steam and fuel pressure gauges were situated above the fuel tank. At a selling price of £48 and maximum speed of 40–45mph (64–72kph), the Pearson Cox was the last steam motorcycle to be manufactured in any number, and only isolated experimental models have been produced since.

Early motorcyclists were not helped by road conditions of the time

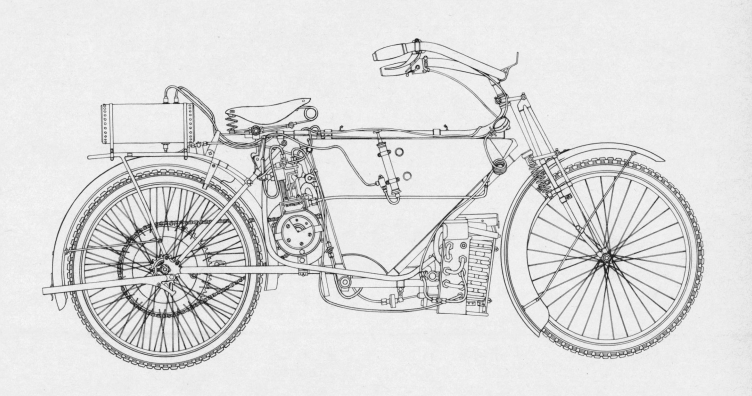

3hp Pearson-Cox steam bicycle, 1912

1913 3½hp Matchless TT Motorcycle

The Collier brothers, Charlie and Harry, became famous on their Matchless motorcycles at Brooklands and the Isle of Man, whilst a third member of the racing team, H. V. Colver, won the Circuit De L'Eure in 1914. The illustrated motorcycle is an ex-works Tourist Trophy machine, one of a small batch built by Harry Collier and Sons Ltd, especially for racing. The engine was of MAG manufacture (Motosacoche of Geneva) a V-twin cyclinder giving a cubic capacity of 496cc. The cylinder heads were of the overhead valve type, and push-rod-operated valves set at an angle of 45° were an unusual feature in such early days. In its original form this model was equipped with an AMAL carburettor, Armstrong three-speed gear hub in the rear wheel and direct belt drive, but punishment meted out by the 3½hp engine was far too excessive for the intricate mechanism, and the hub was a constant source of trouble. It was replaced by a separate Enfield, two-speed gear-box with clutch and all-chain drive, which was a better fitment as this motorcycle liked to run at not less than 35–40mph (56–64kph). It was likely to 'run lumpy' at a slower speed owing to the light weight of the revolving parts, and was altogether much happier at speeds in the region of 60–65mph (96–104kph).

The illustrated Matchless was used for sprint trial work after World War I, and is most likely the same machine that was ridden with success by both S. R. Axford and Jimmy Alexander. The Matchless factory is one of the oldest in motorcycling and even though they were a force to reckon with in racing, they relied heavily upon other makes of engine—De Dion, MAG, MMC, and JAP—until the 1920s when their first single and V-twin units were built.

A great deal of concern was expressed during 1913 about the speed of TT racing motorcycles becoming too fast for the Isle of Man course, and suggestions were made that either fuel restrictions be enforced again or engine capacity be limited if not cut down. Serious consideration was given to the idea of holding future TT events at another venue, particularly the 1903 Gordon Bennet course in Ireland. A very superior steamer service across the Irish Sea was another reason for this argument, but finally the organisers decided to improve the existing Isle of Man course. In addition, all TT competitors were urged to wear racing helmets for that year, and a note of urgency was lent to this message when one of the Rudge Whitworth riders met with a fatal accident.

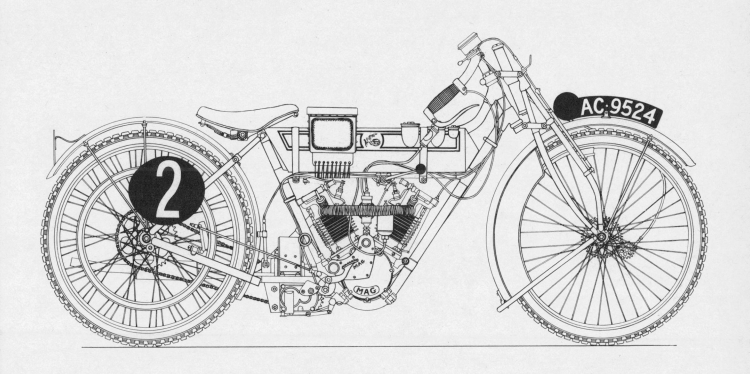

3½hp Matchless TT motorcycle, 1913

1914 1hp Wall Autowheel

This power unit, consisting of wheel and engine, was designed for early attachment alongside the rear wheel of any ordinary pedal-driven bicycle. It was particularly popular with touring cyclists, who found that it helped take much of the ache out of tired legs, especially on long steep hills where they may otherwise have been tempted to get off and push. Patented by Mr A. W. Wall in 1908, and subsequently improved by the makers, BSA, the original Autowheel consisted of a small twin-cylinder, horizontally opposed, two-stroke engine, mounted in a tubular frame with a single 20in (50.8cm) diameter road wheel. The whole unit clamped conveniently onto one side of the rear forks with a throttle control mounted on the handlebar. It was modified the following year and again in 1912, finally becoming, as illustrated, a 1hp single-cylinder, air-cooled motor with outside flywheel and a short chain drive to the road wheel. Later models incorporated a basic form of two-speed gear in the engine crank case, so that much less pedal assistance was required. It cost much less than a motorcycle to buy, and was economical to run, as 1pt (0.57l) lubricating oil was sufficient for 600 miles and $\frac{1}{2}$gal (2.27l) petrol served for 50–60 miles (80–90km), or much more if the rider cared to switch the motor off and revert to leg power whenever the going was easier.

The Autowheel remained popular for many years, not only amongst touring cyclists, but also as a means of propulsion for invalid carriages and small industrial trucks etc. It was also incorporated as the rear wheel of a motor scooter and was made in the USA in a re-designed form during 1915.

1hp Wall Autowheel, 1914

1914 3½hp Scott Motorcycle

Alfred Scott began experimenting with two-stroke engines before the turn of the century, but the first motorcycle bearing his famous name did not appear on the market until 1908. Scott pursued an independent line of development at a time when single-cylinder, four-stroke engines ruled the day, and his first machine, a small parallel-twin two-stroke with a triangulated open cradle-type of frame had little, if any, influence on other motorcycle designers of the time.

Production had moved to Shipley, in Yorkshire, when the little two-speed Scott motorcycle with water-cooled engines really began to excel in sprint events, high speed racing and hill-climb competitions. His machines made the fastest laps on the Isle of Man in 1911, 1912 and 1913, and won the 1912 and 1913 Senior Tourist Trophy races. In 1912 Frank Appleby and Frank Philipp had led the race nearly all the way on 500cc Scott two-strokes. Philipp was unfortunately detained by a puncture, but Appleby streaked home in first place about six minutes in front of the following Triumph, despite a faulty brake and troublesome rear stand which had to be kicked back into place once or twice. Because of Scott's success, some rival manufacturers considered the two-stroke, water-cooled engine with rotary valves, had an unfair advantage over the more mechanically complex four-strokes, and they did their best to have the Scotts penalised. Nevertheless, Tim Woods won the 1913 Senior event on his Scott after a long hard tussle with Indian and Rudge, but in the following year's race the Scott's lead was spoiled by a faulty magneto, and Cyril Pullin came through to win on a Rudge-Multi.

The Scott's growing reputation for smoothness and stability, as well as racing success and its inevitable publicity, led to a more general acceptance of this unorthodox design and eventually to a wider adoption of the two-stroke principle. Alfred Scott made a small fortune before selling his interest in the firm during 1919, leaving a small band of fellow Yorkshiremen to continue the company's high standard of workmanship. Against a successful production backcloth of 500cc and 600cc twins, Squirrels, Super-Squirrels, and Flying Squirrels, they proceeded to develop prototype single, V-twin and three-cylinder engines, but generally Scott motorcycles followed the original pattern. Even the 'new' Scotts of the mid 1920s, with extended TT tank and three-speed gearbox, were not so very different in appearance, and with periodic improvement they continued right into the post-war years. Alfred Scott died in 1923 having unsuccessfully tried to promote the Scott Sociable cycle car, an unorthodox three-wheeler which, in appearance, resembled a covered-in motorcycle with sidecar.

3½hp Scott motorcycle, 1914

1914 976cc BAT Motorcycle

The BAT Manufacturing Co (who's slogan was 'best after tests') were renowned for their spring-framed, large V-twin cylinder motorcycles. They originally built this machine for use at Brooklands, and when it was later equipped for the road, the 976cc JAP engine and three-speed, close-ratio, Sturmey-Archer gearbox with hand-change lever were retained. The round-section fuel tank contained oil in a front compartment and petrol at the rear, and was furnished, on the outside, with a manually operated oil pump and rubber pads against which the rider located his knees. Special BAT features included extra strengthening stays running outside of the rear forks from spindle to crank case, and a wheel spindle at the front attached to a coil-spring-supported, U-shaped arm. Vibration had been a particular annoyance for the early motorcyclists, but the successful development of spring forks—notably the Druid design of 1906—had made things much more comfortable for the rider. The frame, petrol tank, speedometer, fittings and bottom half of the engine were identical to the less powerful BAT model, the 770cc Light Roadster. Originally designed by T. H. Tessier,

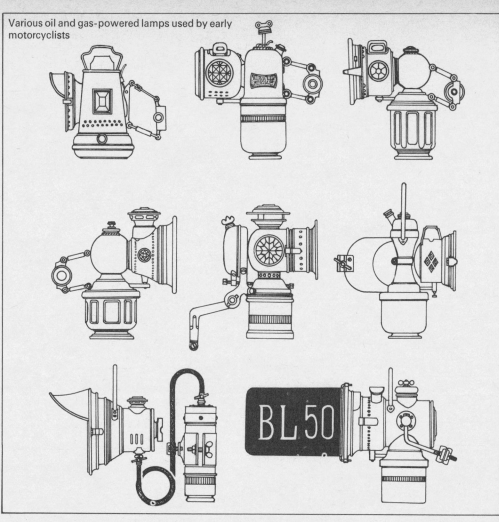

Various oil and gas-powered lamps used by early motorcyclists

BAT motorcycles were sporting single-cylinder engines in spring frames from 1903, and over the following years, JAP V-twin engines of various capacity were installed.

These machines successfully competed in the Isle of Man TT, Brooklands and other international races until the firm's closure during the mid 1920s.

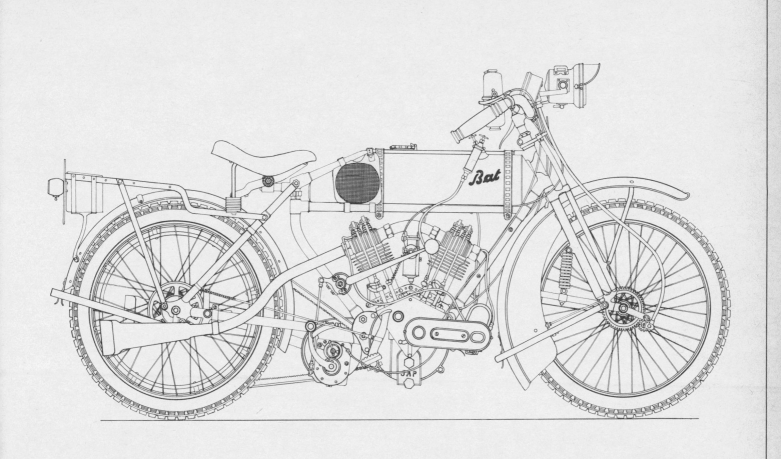

976cc BAT motorcycle, 1914

1914 350cc Elswick Motorcycle

A number of firms such as Sunbeam, BSA, Rudge, Triumph, James, Premier, and Norton, designed specialist power units, and there were also numerous proprietary engines from Minerva, MAG, Blackburne, Peugeot, Prestwich, and others for the smaller motorcycle factories to adopt. The illustrated machine, made by the Elswick Cycle and Manufacturing Co, Barton-on-Humber, in Lincolnshire, had a Birmingham-produced, 350cc, Junior Precision engine with camshaft-operated valves behind the cylinder, a German design VH magneto and a non-automatic Brown and Barlow carburettor, in which each movement of the gas lever necessitated an adjustment on the air lever to keep the mixture correct. Engine lubrication was by a manually-operated, spring-loaded pump on top of the fuel tank, with the oil carried separately in a small compartment at the front, as was customary at this time. With this lubrication system, the pump plunger had to be pushed down by hand from where it moved slowly back up under spring pressure, forcing the oil through a pipe to an inlet on the front of the crank case, where it dropped onto the big end as it was turning, and splashed about lubricating gears and bearings. It was important that the rider frequently checked, through a glass sighter, the amount of lubricant going into the engine, and adjusted the flow rate to its requirements. When the plunger reached the top of its stroke he had to remember to push it down again immediately or there would be no oil going into the mechanism. Another disadvantage with this system was its inclination to syphon if the engine stopped with the valves in a certain position, and many an unsuspecting owner returned to find all the oil gone from the tank into the crank case. The days when forgetful motorcyclists ruined an engine through lack of oil, or gummed up the exhaust with excess, were soon forgotten when mechanically-operated pressure-lubrication systems were adopted towards the 1920s. This Elswick model was also equipped with two gears, and belt drive to the rear wheel. A lever on the right handlebar operated the front brake, a pull-up stirrup type as used on push bikes, and virtually useless except as a 'bobby dodger'. They caused a great many accidents by snatching or coming loose, but a front brake was required by law. The rear brake was operated by the left heel and acted on the outside of the belt rim, which fortunately was more efficient. This dangerous state of affairs remained unchanged for some time, and even during the twenties when motorcar braking improved by leaps and bounds, that on motorcycles remained much as it was before World War I.

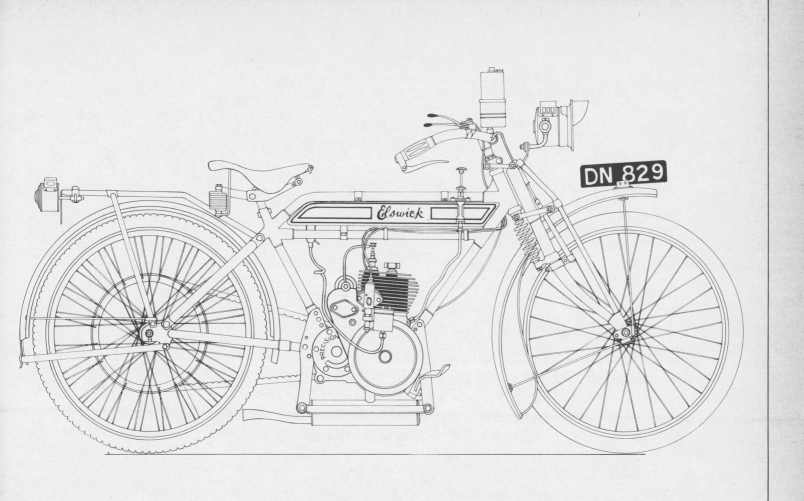

350cc Elswick motorcycle, 1914

1915 11hp American Militaire Motorcycle

Following World War I, manufacturers in Europe found the four-cylinder formula too costly to build, and also unduly complicated when compared with the simpler but efficient single and twin-cylinder motorcycles then available. The advantage of power and weight offered by the four-cylinder formula, was far more appropriate in places like the USA, where greater distances and more varied terrain had to be covered.

The 11hp, four-cylinder American Militaire made its first appearance in 1915, having been developed as a vehicle for heavy sidecar work, particularly in the field of military warfare. The underslung, pressed-steel frame, patented three years earlier, when the machine was equipped with a steering wheel instead of handlebars, provided a low centre of gravity, and together with a longer than usual wheelbase (65in : 165.1cm) it offered a great deal of stability for the rider. The four-cylinder, overhead-valve, air-cooled motor was built on automobile principles with an enclosed fly wheel, dry plate clutch, and four-speed gearbox, with a car-style gear change lever bolted onto the engine case and forming a solid unit. Shaft drive to the rear wheel was used. Further equipment included a self starter, foot-operated brake lever, electric head and tail lights, horn, and tool chest. The machine turned on a pivoted front axle and was kept upright by the small stabiliser wheels on the rear axle. They were raised by a small foot lever when the vehicle was under way and lowered again when running in congested districts. Thus the rider need never place his foot on the ground. Two unusual features included on this motorcycle were the reverse gear, and the 28in (71.1cm) artillery-style wheels.

Official observers from the British Army were present at the TT and other racing events in 1912, and during the same year a special series of trials were carried out over all manner of rough ground in order to determine which makes of motorcycle were most able to cope with battlefield conditions. The War Department was, however, very slow to realise the true potential of motorcycles for general military duties and therefore, when war broke out in 1914, the experienced men who answered the emergency call for dispatch riders with the British Expeditionary Force, were initially mounted on various makes of second-hand machines, until the Army was able to standardise with Douglas and Triumph, and the Royal Flying Corps, with P & M.

The Motorcycle Machine-gun Corps, was formed in 1915, some three years after Scotts had exhibited $3\frac{3}{4}$hp, solo model, with a machine-gun attached to the handlebars, at the Olympia Show. The MMGC favoured Clyno and Royal Enfield V-twins with armoured sidecars and Vickers' machine-guns, while some Scott and Matchless machines were also employed in a similar role. Alfred Scott designed a built-in-one Guncar with a three-wheeled arrangement similar to that of a sidecar outfit. The suspension was better and the whole thing more robust, but the contract with the War Office he hoped for, failed to materialise. A modified version came out after the war, but this time it was called the Scott Sociable—an unorthodox-looking, three-wheeled, enclosed runabout for two people. Peacetime saw a great revival in the motorcycle trade, but the boom brought with it a rash of cheap and unsound designs, as established and new manufacturers competed against each other for the market.

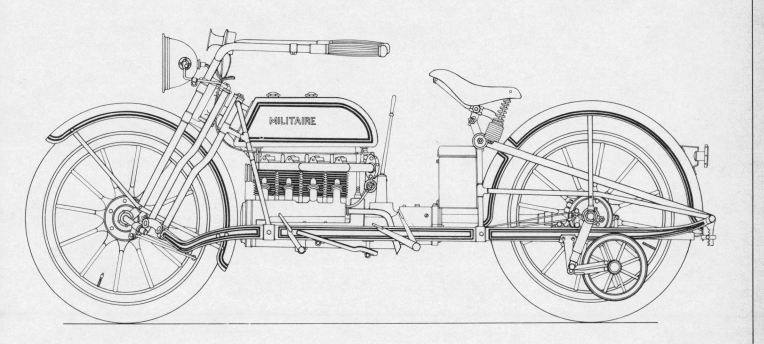

11hp American Militaire motorcycle, 1915

1915 3½hp Rudge Multi Motorcycle

Manufactured by Rudge Whitworth Ltd, of Coventry, this single-cylinder, belt-driven motorcycle incorporated the highly successful, variable speed transmission produced by the makers in 1911 for their private-owner TT machines. The gear ranged from 3.5:1 to 7:1 and consisted of variable belt pulleys on the engine shaft and rear wheel, the one increasing in diameter as the other decreased, so that the drive belt was kept at a constant tension and a smooth change of gear obtained. This arrangement resulted in an unusually long gear lever, and a clumsy-looking rear wheel pulley, but the gear proved highly successful and Rudge machines so equipped had the Rudge Multi emblem on the petrol tank. The epicyclic-hub gear was the most popular form of multi-speed gearing on road-going machines at this time, and was generally used in conjunction with a free engine clutch, so that the machine could be pedal started with the rear wheel up on a stand. Originally developed for pedal cycles, this type of gearing was too fragile and intricate for motorcycle use, but it served the purpose until three and four-speed, countershaft gearboxes were adopted, after 1914.

Unit construction of engine and gear-box also began to feature about this time. The Rudge-Whitworth engine, with Senspray carburettor and CAV magneto, was set vertically in the frame and employed an inlet-over-exhaust valve arrangement similar to the Indian engine. The petrol tank was arranged with all the fittings together on one side, in order to facilitate easy removal from the frame, and a separate oil tank was carried on the saddle stem. These flat slab-shaped petrol tanks had hardly changed since the early years. They had served well, but were inadequate for racing as the distances became longer, so a rounded form of tank, which straddled the top frame tube was adopted by the speed men. Besides having twice the capacity, the new saddle-tanks were more streamlined and comfortable, and although some manufacturers resisted until the end, they also became standard on touring models by the end of the 1920s.

Rudge Whitworth gained a fine reputation before World War II for their range of engines, some of which had four valves, as well as for the multi-gear. A 500cc Rudge victory in the 1914 Senior TT with Cyril Pullin riding, was the first on a list of sporting achievements up to the late 1930s, when the company closed.

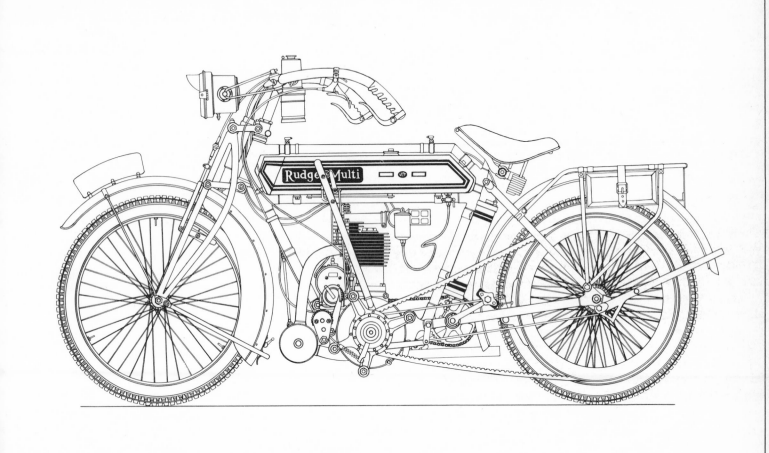

3½hp Rudge Multi motorcycle, 1915

1916   1¾hp Autoped Scooter

Originating from the Autoped Co of New York, this early scooter was produced for a short time in England by Imperial Motor Industries Ltd. The cause of commerical failure may have been its suitability for short journeys only, as no seating or weather protection was provided for the driver, who stood balanced precariously on a narrow platform behind the battery box. Whatever the reason, it certainly was not the complexity of its controls, as the handlebar column was simply raised to engage the single speed, and dropped to disengage. The brakes were also applied by movements of the same column. It was powered by a 162cc, four-stroke engine, with a flywheel magneto and floatless carburettor, and this make of scooter was also available with an electric motor driving the front wheel, and batteries carried in the box on the platform.

By 1912 several more motorcycle manufacturers had ladies' models on the market, all with an open type of frame and an abundance of protection over the rear wheel and the drive belt, to prevent petticoats, skirts, and other items of female apparel from becoming entangled. There was a much bigger market for two-wheelers amongst women after World War I, by which time the fair sex were displaying an increasing interest in motorcycle sport. Contemporary photographs taken at Brooklands, the Isle of Man, and local trial events, indicate that almost as many ladies as gentlemen enjoyed the occasions, whilst a growing number of them were beginning to compete in reliability trials, and not surprisingly, they soon proved able to ride at speed with skill of which anyone might be proud There was a short-lived craze for scooters in the 1920s, when all manner of means were used by makers to attract women customers, from finishing in attractive colours, to putting on solid rubber tyres so that they were free of worries about tyre punctures or blow outs. Scooters were not meant to be fast, as women rarely sought after high speed. They were simply an economical and convenient way to travel to lunch, make social calls, or take a spin through the countryside without having to dress like a deep-sea fisherman.

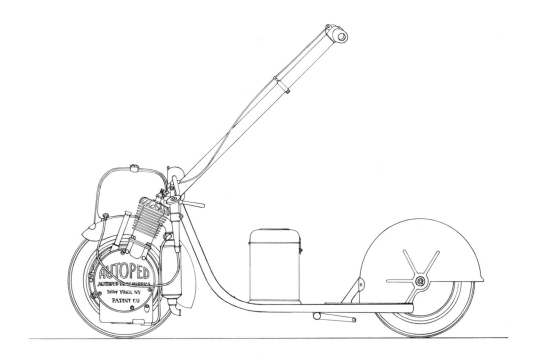

1¾hp Autoped scooter, 1916

1917 5/6hp Clyno-Vickers Machine-gun Combination

Although the use of motorcycles for military purposes dates from the late nineteenth century, they were not able to fulfil a major role until World War I erupted in Europe. Pre-war motorcycle enthusiasts then came forward to be trained as army dispatch riders, and were soon put to work mounted upon Triumph, BSA, Douglas, P & M, Sunbeam and Norton models. On the battlefield the machine-gun was proving to be a most devastating weapon, and the British Army further increased its use by forming the Machine-gun Corps in October 1915. The MGC consisted of three sections, two of which supported the infantry and cavalry, while a third section, the Motor Machine-gun Corps, was more mobile. It had been decided to equip this branch with motorcycle combinations, and extensive trials were then carried out to determine the most suitable motorcycle and sidecar for war service. The award went to Clyno for their 5/6hp and 8hp, three-speed combinations, as they were not only considered to be of advanced design, but the easily removable V-twin engine, inter-changeable wheels, enclosed final drive and three-point sidecar suspension, made them exceedingly practical for service use. However, some 3¾hp Scott, Matchless and Royal Enfield motorcycle com-binations were also employed as machine-gun carriers.

The Clyno carried a Vickers' machine-gun and armoured shield, attached to the sidecar chassis by a tripod mount. The gun would normally point forwards, but when necessary, it could be swivelled to the reverse direction. A simple seat was provided for the gunner on the floor of the sidecar, whilst boxes of spare ammunition, replacement gun parts, a container of water for the gun cooling system, petrol, oil and carbide for the lamps were strapped up behind. The gun was seldom, if ever, fired whilst the combination was in motion, and when required it could easily be detached from its mounting and used in a ground firing position. A motorcycle machine-gun section consisted of six Clyno combinations—two had guns, another two, without guns but with armoured shields, served as reserve gun carriers, while the third pair carried spare ammunition and equipment only. The section was completed by an officer and NCO on solo motorcycles. Clynos provided with normal passenger sidecars, were used by the British and the Allies throughout the war, after which the Clyno firm produced single and V-twins before going over to the manufacture of motorcars in 1923. Motorcycles were used extensively by all European and American combatants during World War I, especially for scouting and dispatch rider work.

5/6hp Clyno-Vickers machine-gun combination, 1917

1918 Sunbeam Motorcycle

In 1912 John Marsden produced the first motorcycle under his firm's old trade mark of Sunbeam. He had earlier been successful as a pedal cycle maker, and in 1901 had brought out the Sunbeam Mabely motorcar, designed by Mr Mabely Smith, powered by De Dion engine, and steered by tiller from the rear seat. This vehicle proved to be very popular, and two were built every week until the factory was given over to motorcycle production in 1912. Mr Marsden's new 350cc motorcycle, designed by J. E. Greenwood, had a single-cylinder, air-cooled engine, two-speed countershaft gear-box, hand-operated clutch, and featured fully enclosed chain drive working in oil-baths—a Sunbeam feature for many years afterwards.

The design and workmanship of this quiet 350cc motorcycle was unsurpassed, and its finish luxurious— it was even embellished with genuine gold leaf. It was a machine for the connoisseur, but it was still rugged enough to ascend Ben Nevis as a publicity venture. The company introduced a new three-speed 500cc single in 1913 and then, following the trend in motorcycle design, introduced a big twin model, powered by a 770cc, side valve JAP engine, for sidecar work.

Sunbeam's reputation for design and finish continued to flourish, and in 1914 their racing machines began to show a little of the promise which they were to eventually realise in full when the firm's rider, Howard Davies, surprisingly rode his TT Sunbeam into dead-heat second place with O. C. Godfrey's Indian. TT racing was interrupted by World War I, during which 3½hp Sunbeam motorcycles with belt and enclosed-chain drive were supplied on a small scale to the Allies. Unfortunately, John Marsden did not live long enough to see the first post-war TT races of 1920, in which Tommy De la Hay won the Senior event at 51.48mph (82.85kph) on a SV Sunbeam, beating Duggie Brown's Norton by 3½ minutes. In the same race W. R. Brown, also on a Sunbeam, came in third, whilst the Sunbeam of sprint star George Dance was forced out by mechanical trouble after a record lap of 56mph (90.1kph). The 1921 French Grand Prix and the 1922 TT race were both taken by Alec Bennett on a SV 'Longstroke' Sunbeam, which also completed the fastest lap of 59.99mph (96.54kph). This was the last year in which the TT was won by a SV machine, and although SV engines were produced for some years by the company, both their Junior and Senior racing teams used 350cc Sunbeam OHV designs for the following year's race, which George Dance nearly 'had in the bag', only to be stopped by a broken valve a few miles from the finish. Although he narrowly missed winning the Ulster Grand Prix, Charlie Dodson won the Isle of Man TT in both 1928 and 1929, roaring round the second time at 72mph (115.9kph) to create a new lap record for Sunbeam and beat his previous year's time by almost 10mph (16kph).

During World War II, the company was taken over by BSA, but continued to produce under their own name until 1957, when they disappeared from the list of manufacturers. The late 1940s saw Ealing Poppe's impressive design for Sunbeam's 'car on two wheels', in which the accent was on power and comfort, with 500cc, OHV, in-line engine, shaft drive, fully sprung frame, and oversize 'balloon' tyres. The last Sunbeam motorcycle was the S7 model of 1950.

Sunbeam motorcycle, 1918

1919 500cc Indian Power Plus Motorcycle

The Indian Co, was founded in 1900 when George M. Hendee, a pedal cycle maker, joined forces with Oscar Hedstrom. In the following year Hedstrom designed the first prototype Indian motorcycle, basically a heavy type of pedal bicycle with a $1\frac{3}{4}$hp, single-cylinder engine located vertically on the saddle tube, and a petrol tank over the rear wheel. It performed successfully and went into production in 1902 when 143 were made, and the original design was produced until 1905, when it was superseded by a $2\frac{1}{4}$hp model. Improvements were made continually, twist-grip engine control and chain drive being included during the early years. The famous Indian V-twin models, for which the American market was to show strong preference, were first introduced in 1905 using two $1\frac{3}{4}$hp cylinders. Mechanically operated inlet valves were included on all Indian power units from 1908, and the single's power was increased again to $3\frac{1}{2}$hp.

This forward-looking company exported motorcycles to Europe and Britain, and they were distributed under the direction of famous racer, Billy Wells, who along with rider Jake de Rosier, was soon responsible for Indian's string of sporting successes. The year 1911 saw O. C. Godfrey lead an Indian team, mounted on $3\frac{1}{2}$hp twin-cylinder machines, into the first three places of the Senior TT race over Snaefell: C. B. Franklin was second and A. Moorhouse (victim of the first fatal crash at Brooklands soon afterwards) was third. A few years later during World War I, powerful 7/9hp models with sidecar attachment were used for military transport. As the motorcar enjoyed a rapid increase in both development and use, so the popularity of motorcycling began to fade in America, and as the overall number of motorcycle manufacturers there decreased quite rapidly, so such firms as Indian, Harley Davidson, and American Excelsior, further consolidated their positions at the top of the market. But they had to modify their designs to compete with the automobile, and it was the large capacity V-twin, which became the most distinctive of American types, that halted the decline of these firms.

The Indian Powerplus of 1916, emphasised the sporting side of motorcycling, as its 1,000cc side-valve, twin-cylinder engine with gear-box was not only more powerful than the previous V-twin, but it was also equipped with such refinements as an electric starter, electric lighting and cradle-spring frame, designed to give a comfortable ride over the roughest of terrain. Despite the powerful engine, there was no front brake provided, but stopping was almost assured by a dual braking system on the rear wheel, operated separately by hand lever and foot pedal. The sporting Powerplus engine could be obtained in a rigid frame by those who preferred it to the leaf-spring version, whilst a sidecar attachment made a smart combination with either model. Finished in the familiar red with gold script on the tank side, as were all Indian motorcycles after 1910, the Powerplus was superseded by the Indian Chief in 1921. Soon afterwards, the company used their Scout model as the basis for a hotted-up 750cc Police Special, said to be capable of 75–80mph (120–128kph).

500cc Indian Powerplus motorcycle, 1919

1919 1hp ABC Skootamota

The first post-war years saw an amazing growth in the number of manufacturers of small two-stroke motorcycles and small-wheeled machines, nicknamed 'scooters'. One of the earliest of this kind was the compact, single-cylinder, 125cc, ABC Skootamota, designed by Granville Bradshaw. He arranged its lightweight, tubular framework in open form with a wide, slightly curving footboard across the centre, steering-head handlebars to the fore, and battery box and driver's seat at the rear. The small four-stroke motor, a highly efficient OHV air-cooled, 125cc unit, was positioned horizontally over the rear wheel to which it was connected by a single chain and sprockets. A combined petrol and oil tank was placed neatly above the horizontal engine with magneto at one end and short exhaust to silencer at the other. The 15in (38.1cm) diameter wheels were both fitted with external contracting brakes, operated by hand and foot levers. Numerous other makes of scooter became available about this time and were praised for their usefulness and simplicity, but this form of vehicle was not widely adopted until after 1945.

By the early 1920s there was a growing demand for passenger-carrying machines. Generally increased engine power enabled motorcycles of 250cc and above to cope with a sidecar outfit, and within a few years there was a range of designs available to suit all tastes and pockets. The sporting sidecars sacrificed comfort for the sake of a streamlined appearance. They were built on the lines of the TT models (sidecar TT races took place in 1923, 1924 and 1925) and were octagonal in section like an airship, with a pointed tail built of polished aluminium or polished mahogany, with metal beading around the edges. Some manufacturers such as Coventry Eagle, made sidecars to match their petrol tanks. Development of chassis and body construction made touring sidecars more attractive as the decade progressed. The family man was able to choose his attachment from a wide variety of models in which every consideration had been given to full weather protection and passenger comfort. The days of backbreaking, neck-cricking journeys in the freezing cold were becoming a thing of the past, as both adult and child passengers could watch the miles speed by from the luxury of reclining seats with the additional comfort of a solid-fuel foot warmer—a far cry from the first models placed on the market by Mills & Fulford in 1903.

Motorcycle taxis enjoyed a brief vogue about 1920, but the limited passenger capacity was the biggest drawback with them. Motorcycles with sidecars became popular for trade purposes in Britain, whilst specialist three-wheelers from the German Zündap and DKW factories were adopted on the continent as light delivery vans. BSA proposed to resurrect the detachable forecar, popularised at the beginning of the century as the Phoenix Trimo, and update it as a tradesman's box, an idea that proved to be quite successful with delivery and street salesmen.

As the sidecar went into a decline towards 1930 due to the growing availability of small cars, the pillion seat, or 'flapper bracket', grew in popularity. Pillion passengers were carried on motorcycles for years before any proper provision was made for their safety and comfort. A rolled-up cushion strapped to the carrier was the usual arrangement for a longish journey, with the passenger, if she were a young lady, sitting side-saddle without foot-rest support. Motorcycles were somewhat difficult to steer and control anyway, without the additional weight of an unbalance passenger, and the danger remained until the general adoption of sprung pillion seats and the astride position during the 1920s.

1hp ABC Skootamota, 1919

1919 1,000cc Indian Daytona Motorcycle

During the early years of this century in America, large crowds were attracted to the velodromes by pedal cycle racing, but promoters soon went one better, and in 1908 the first motorcycle board-racing track was built in New Jersey by an engineer named Jack Prince. Soon each major American city sported a similar 'motordrome', and spectacular competitions were organised on a national league basis. Although riding the boards was safer than the small horse tracks, which threw up clouds of choking dust, terrific rivalry between professional riders, doubtful team tactics and the much faster speeds, resulted in a high casualty rate and frequent death. The oval board tracks varied in distance between $\frac{1}{4}$-$\frac{1}{3}$ mile (although a few were longer) but all were steeply banked on the bends to encourage high speeds. The pine timbers forming the track surface, were layed as flush as possible, with especially careful blending on the bends, but the boards could not be planed smooth or the motorcycle tyres would not grip. The fragile-looking mounts lapped at speeds approaching 90mph (115kph) whilst the crowds of spectators looked down on team events over the rim of the bowl. Riders wore little protection other than leathers, and whoever came adrift collected at least a mass of splinters. Often the boards became rotten and split, or were saturated with engine oil blown out by the countless exhausts. The tremendous speeds and centrifugal force on the bends often sent riders dizzy, and out-of-control machines piled into the spectators. Death and injury had reached such a pitch by 1913 that the authorities called a halt to 'motordrome madness', and the sensation-seeking spectators were forced to look elsewhere. However, board racing switched to larger and safer 1 and 2-mile board tracks after the World War I, when three-figure speeds were achieved.

The illustrated 1919 Indian Motorcycle had a fast, V-twin, 1,000cc, Daytona engine packed into a slender frame. It had no clutch, wheelguards or brakes, and is typical of the machines which roared around the ovals until the time of the great depression.

1,000cc Indian Daytona motorcycle, 1919

1919 500cc Brough Flat-twin

William Edward Brough, born in 1861, worked for a number of years as a steam-engine mechanic and foreman electrician at Cinderhill colliery, Nottingham, England, before moving to Basford, in Nottinghamshire, where he started a business of his own in 1899. Although his engineering experience was mainly concerned with steam power, he had inventiveness and vision enough to see himself as a manufacturer of motorcars and motorcycles, which were then coming into use. He commenced business by producing a small belt-driven car with a $3\frac{1}{2}$hp De Dion engine.

The first Brough motorcycle was available in 1902, and had a pedal-cycle-type frame with a small engine mounted in an unusual position in front of, and below the bottom bracket, with belt drive to the rear wheel and pedals to assist the engine on hills. Very soon the firm was able to make nearly all of its own frame and engine parts, as well as providing for other manufacturers in the expanding trade. By 1908 the design of William Brough's motorcycle was much improved and the power increased to $3\frac{1}{2}$hp.

The famous W. E. Brough flat or horizontally opposed twin-cylinder models were built from 1911, and one of his sons, George, who later designed and produced the exclusive Brough Superior motorcycle as a separate venture, rode a flat twin in the 1913 senior TT race, and on numerous occasions, with success, in the London to Edinburgh trials. Brough production centred around the 500cc and 692cc horizontally opposed twin-cylinder models, with 3-speed Sturmey Archer gear-box mounted beneath the rear cylinder, and a small number of larger 810cc flat twins, until the company ceased business in 1925.

Motorcyclists of the day were keen to put their mounts through the most rigorous tests in order to prove their reliability. Some of these trials, such as the Scottish Six Day, covered as many as 400 miles of terrain where vehicles never ordinarily ventured. Cart tracks, water-splashes and blinding rain and snow were endured by the rider as he endeavoured to prove the merits of a machine, which in the first place was not designed for cross-country work. Trials were arranged by local clubs everywhere, and at the weekend enthusiasts donned their 'oilies' and set off to tackle several miles of rough stuff. The anti-motorcycling brigade, and newspapers in particular, took a dim view of these antics and issued a distorted account of motorcyclists taking to the footpaths in hoards, and forcing pedestrians onto the highway where they were run down by motorists. By the mid 1920s, motorcyclists were making frequent expeditions to foreign places, crossing continents and inevitably attempting to encircle the globe. The classic test for any rider was the Durban to Johannesburg race. First held in 1913 it ranked as the longest and most strenuous speed trial in the world, over 406 miles (653.4km) of rugged mountain country—excellent propaganda for the early motorcycling movement.

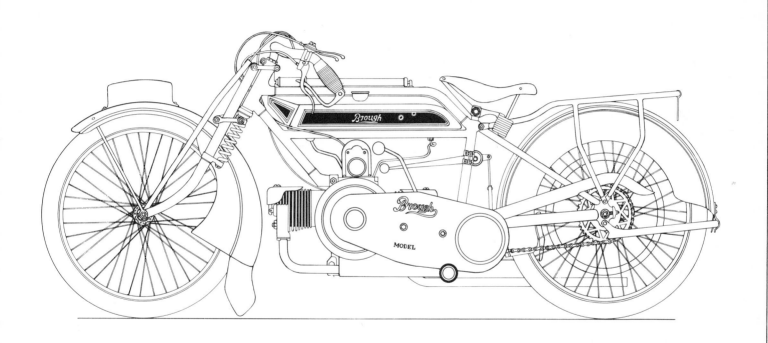

500cc Brough flat-twin, 1919

1920 2½hp Autoglider

The Birmingham-made Autoglider was amongst the more successful designs to be brought out during the short-lived scooter craze of the early 1920s. This proved to be a popular little machine for ladies' shopping trips, because of its well-sprung platform and spacious accommodation for parcels etc, in the seat box. For the price of £40, the purchaser received an open, tubular-frame machine with a Union 292cc engine that consumed about 1gal (0.57l) petrol every 90–100 miles (145–161km), from a tank set between the handlebars. Pottering along in single gear, the rider was assured of comfort through a laminated spring suspension. A choice of models was available, one with a seat and the other without, so that there was space for the driver to stand up and carry a standing passenger behind. But the 1920s was the decade of the sidecar, and motorcyclists who wished to carry a passenger were buying fully sprung sidecar attachments that were almost as comfortable as a motorcar to ride in. A sidecar race was included in the TT competitions during 1923, and it proved to be one of the most thrilling spectacles ever seen on the Isle of Man, but unfortunately the event was abandoned after two years, because it was not considered to be encouraging the design and development of touring outfits.

Sidecar racing continued to flourish at Brooklands and other places however, and it seems there was never any shortage of volunteers to sit 'in the chair' and suffer the danger and discomforts it involved. The passenger's job was to act as ballast, and he was weighed in before the race began, like a jockey, so that speed records could be officially recognised. Out on the track he was required to tuck his legs right up into the point of the torpedo-shaped shell, and lie down flat, so as not to break the windstream. These little unsprung boxes swayed about and seesawed alarmingly at speed with each gear change or acceleration, and the passenger had only a thin iron bar to hang onto. After a few laps of the course he would be battered and bruised about the body from the continuous bouncing of the sidecar wheel, and gradually become so sickened by doses of alcholic fumes from the exhaust, that he was quite likely to pass out before the race had finished.

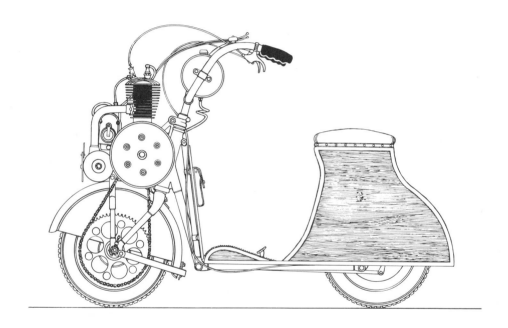

2½hp Autoglider, 1920

1920 490cc SV Norton Motorcycle

James L. Norton, a chain maker from Birmingham, England, started his motorcycle business in 1898 and for some years produced the Clement Energette. Norton's first success came in the twin-cylinder class of the 1907 TT race, when Rem Fowler won on a Peugeot-engined Norton. Although he had a deal of trouble with tyres and drive belt, he averaged 36mph (57.9kph), and completed one non-stop lap at 43mph (69.2kph), before finally finishing a full half-hour in front of Billy Wells on a Vindec.

Machines of entirely Norton manufacture became available with 490cc and 635cc capacity engines, and gained a fine reputation in racing circles, especially when D. R. 'Wizard' O'Donovan started to take records in the 80mph region (129kph) on a single-cylinder, side-valve model similar to the one shown here. This machine was converted from belt to chain drive in 1924, and the frame and petrol tank were shortened in order to improve control. Its high-speed performance was aided by a CAV magneto, AMAC TT carburettor and three-speed TT gear-box. Nortons of $4\frac{1}{2}$hp were produced by the company for Allied troops during World War I, and in the first TT race following the Armistice (1920) Nortons came in second to Sunbeam by $3\frac{1}{2}$ minutes. In the following year, O'Donovan established a new time of 72mph (115.9kph) for the sidecar flying kilometre on a SV model, and about the same time Rex Judd was employed by the Norton works to test ride and provide these machines with a guarantee of having reached 70–75mph (113–121kph) before delivery to customer. Judd specialised in long-distance record-breaking, and also received the Godfrey Cup for being the first 500cc rider to top 90mph (114.8kph).

New overhead-valve models were ousting side-valve designs by 1924, the year in which Norton's run of TT success began with George Tucker taking the sidecar race, and Alec Bennett winning the senior TT. In this race, Bennett set up a new record of 62mph (99.8kph) in front of a large crowd which included, for the last time, old James Norton, who had entered his motorcycles year after year in the hope of repeating Rem Fowler's 1907 victory. Norton's impressive tally of firsts grew to include the Belgian, Ulster, and French Grands Prix, the Spanish twelve-hour race, Brooklands senior 200-mile (322-km) race, Circuit of Cremona, and others, all achieved, as Nortons claimed, on standard engines—just the same as those sold to the public.

The talented Stanley Woods joined the firm in 1926 and won that year's senior TT event on a push-rod Norton at 67.54mph (108.7kph), coming in ahead of Jimmy Simpson, who produced the first TT lap above 70mph (113kph). In 1927 the senior win again went to Alec Bennett, who raced home with an average speed of 68.41mph (110.1kph) on a new 500cc overhead-camshaft model, which Nortons successfully put into production the following year as the CSI, although other leading manufacturers were listing OHC sports models in their catalogue by then. Joe Craig designed Nortons new OHC machine for the 1930 senior race. It was ridden by Jimmy Simpson and beaten into third place by two Rudges, but from then on senior TT events were absolutely dominated by the 'cammy' Nortons, which won during the years 1931–4, 1936–8, 1947–54 and again in 1961. The 1935 and 1939 races were won by the Continentals, Moto Guzzi and BMW respectively.

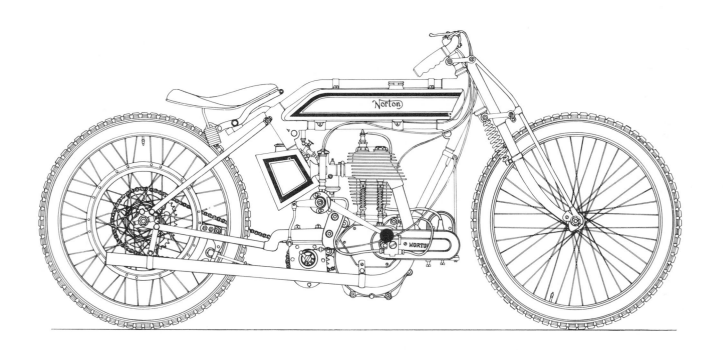

490cc SV Norton motorcycle, 1920

1920 3½hp NUT Motorcycle

There were a variety of V-twin-engined motorcycles on the market by 1920, but none was more handsome or elegant than the twin-cylinder machine made by the British, Newcastle-upon-Tyne Motor Co. It was the personal design of Mr Hugh Mason, an expert engineer and ex-TT rider, who was closely associated with the firm. He drew upon his considerable experience to create a beautiful machine for the use of those riders who required a really fast, ultra-luxurious solo-tourer that might also be suitable for light sidecar work. This belt-driven motorcycle was powered by a 500cc, side-valve engine—only one of the wide range of power units made by JAP especially for NUT motorcycles. It could be purchased complete with Lucas electric lighting set, three-speed gear-box and a very efficient dual braking system, for 140 guineas (£147). This particular manufacturer always paid a great deal of attention to the finish of their models, which were a distinctive nut-brown with gold embellishment, and frequently the engine cylinders were plated to give an even more attractive appearance. The twenties saw a string of well-designed NUT

machines, with increased power, put onto the market for solo and sidecar work. But the demand for powerful, twin-cylinder engines declined, and this Northumberland-based firm was soon forced into closure by the thirties slump.

Between the wars, horse fairs and gymkhanas provided amateur motorcyclists with a chance to demonstrate their trick riding abilities. As well as solo gyrations, there were spectacular team events such as motorcycle chariot racing, sidecar polo, surf riding and stunting, whilst the one-armed rider Eric Peacock entertained the Brooklands crowd by making ascents of the test hill, long jumping his machine over barrels, and riding around a circle at 5mph (8kph) facing his rear wheel. By the mid 1920s there was already keen contention for the world motorcycle long jump record, then set at 62ft (18.9m) by South African rider, Piet Lievaart. Americans were amusing themselves by travelling long distances at the lowest possible speed, whilst in England, motorcycle football was all the rage—not a dangerous game when played by experts, but novices were quite likely to ride over the ball and burst it. Another motorcycle sport that caught on in England was known as freak hill climbing. This was introduced from

America, and the first event held at Kingsclere, Berkshire, in 1925. All that was required was a big steep hill, impossibly covered by nettles, rabbit holes and flints of various sizes. Riders or 'slant artists' raced one by one for the top, against the clock, but their bucking, pitching bikes seldom reached it and were far more likely to run backwards or somersault down the slope. Grass track racing, on smooth oval tracks, was also established about this time.

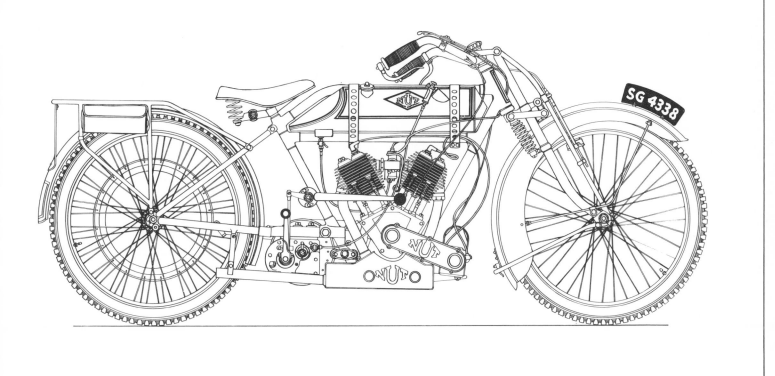

3½hp NUT motorcycle, 1920

1920 350cc Pullin-Groome Motorcycle

Patented in 1920 by ex-TT rider Cyril Pullin and S. L. Groome, the Pullin-Groome motorcycle broke away from established principles competely. Their unorthodox lightweight model, with its excellent weather protection, had an open type of frame consisting of pressed steel plates welded together and incorporating fuel tanks for 9pt (5.1l) petrol and 4pt (2.3l) oil in the upper part, with space for the engine below. The horizontal, 350cc, two-stroke engine of their own design was fully enclosed except for a detachable cylinder head, but doors were provided in the frame sides to allow easy access for crank case and flywheel inspection etc. Both front and rear forks were hinged to telescopic spring tubes, and retained easily detachable, inter-changeable wheels with knock-out spindles. The single-engine cylinder, cast in one with the crank case, was mounted horizontally in the frame, pointing in a forwards direction. Pullin dispensed with a conventional carburettor and instead used a hand-operated mixing valve on the cylinder head. Drive from the engine to rear wheel was all chain, through a two-speed epicycle gear. The rear wheel was served by two independent brakes—one operated by a handlebar lever, the other by foot pedal—and a flywheel magneto provided ignition and lighting current. Despite its advanced design, the Pullin-Groome was dogged by financial problems, and production ceased in 1925.

Cyril Pullin tried again a few years later with another scooter-like design, the 496cc Ascot-Pullin. This also had a pressed steel body, good all-weather protection, with windshield and wiper, as well as hydraulic brakes. But even at the bargain price of £75, its advanced design failed to attract enough customers, and production ceased after only two years.

Several enclosed and semi-enclosed designs appeared on the market during the 1920s, but the Ner-a-Car, of American origin, was the only one to achieve popularity. Wheel discs came and went as a point of fashion, but lingered on sidecar outfits and cycle cars. Specialist firms making weather-protection devices and clothing for motorcyclists did a good trade alongside the mainstream of the industry. By 1927 the choice of motorcycles on the British market had become pleasantly bewildering for the prospective purchaser, as there were no fewer than 598 different models to choose from, ranging between the little single-speed 247cc Radco, priced at £27 1s (£27.5) and the superbly finished, three-speed OHV, 980cc Brough Superior at £195. But the years of depression were only just around the corner, and the picture changed quite drastically. There were 200 firms in Britain alone making motorcycles in the early 1920s, but th number had declined to only 40 manufacturers of significance by the early 1930s. The situation in America was even worse, where only 3 producers were left in business. Chea cars were coming out making motorir possible for everyone. They were reliable and could convey a small family in safety and comfort at 40mph (64kph) so people purchased them in preference to motorcycle combination and after all, they only occupied the same amount of garage space. With this collapse of the market, motorcycl makers concentrated on building fast racers and sports machines.

350cc Pullin-Groome motorcycle, 1920

1920 1½hp Alvis Auto-scooter (Stafford Pup)

The Alvis Motor Co, famous for their motorcars, had limited success when they introduced a line of scooters during the early twenties. Their Stafford Pup, with its standing driving position, only had small appeal to the prospective customer looking for a means of personal transport. The 142cc, single-cylinder, OHV engine straddled the front wheel and unbalanced the machine, making steerage exceptionally heavy. The single cylinder was on one side of the wheel, its flywheel on the other side and the fuel tank directly above, in the centre.

Outside of the luxury and sporting market, motorcycle styling at this time was generally uninspired and angular. Sleeker lines returned later in the decade, when the corners were rounded off on petrol tanks, and exhaust systems were arranged to sweep long and low. A livelier use of colours was made possible by the introduction of cellulose finishes instead of the time-honoured finish of paint and varnish, although the art of intricate lining disappeared from tank sides, frame members and mudguards. Brighter colour schemes were particularly prominent on racers, and the fastest machine of the decade at Brooklands was Claude Temple's, Temple-Anzani, with purple tank and yellow wheels. Chromium plating appeared towards the end of the vintage era and completely supplanted nickel during the early 1930s. Frame design underwent a major transition in those areas where emphasis was placed on comfort and weather protection. Enclosed designs had a run of popularity and then lost their appeal, but the use of steel pressings in place of normal frame tubes persisted here and there for reasons of economy.

Sales of motorcycles increased steadily as the decade progressed with a seemingly endless range of four-stroke, two-stroke, V-twin and flat-twin designs. Specifications were improved all round, countershaft gear-boxes became standard, except on lightweight models, and belt drive was almost totally replaced by chain. Overhead-valve engines began to gain a reputation for power and performance, being supplied in proprietary form by Blackburne and JAP. Meanwhile, across the Atlantic, the American industry was reduced to only three companies—Indian, Harley Davidson, and Excelsior—by recession and a flood of cheap motorcars.

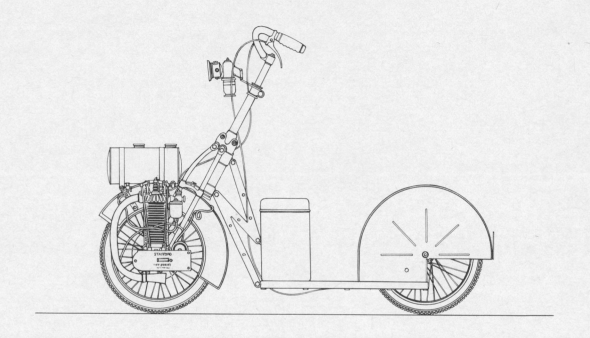

1½hp Alvis auto-scooter, 1920

1921 2½hp Levis Motorcycle

For many years, Levis were amongst the leaders of British motorcycle production, and the two-stroke models, made by Messrs Butterfield at Stechford, Birmingham, were renowned for simplicity, reliability, and quality of workmanship. They were pioneers in the lightweight, two-stroke world and produced a prototype, small capacity, air-cooled engine in 1910. This formed a basis for the lightweight (approximately 100lb [45kg]) 2½hp Levis motorcycle which became extremely popular over the following decade, and whose wide appeal lay in simple specifications, easy maintenance and reasonable purchase price of 33 guineas (£34.65). This 211cc, single-cylinder engine had direct belt drive to the rear wheel, with 5 :1 ratio, and no gears. It was renowned for easy starting, and simply required the rider to push and jump on or pedal away with his legs. Once the engine was turning over, the motorcycle would cruise at approximately 30mph (48kph) with an economical fuel consumption of at least 120mpg (42.5kpl). Petrol and oil tanks contained 1gal and 1pt respectively, and lubrication was by drip-feed to the main bearing and cylinder.

Levis were influential in establishing the lightweight movement of the motorcycling world, and their 2½hp and 2¾hp engines gained a high reputation in Tourist Trophy races of 1913, 1914, 1920, 1921 and 1922. They also produced some interesting prototype engines, including a vertical-twin in 1913 and a flat, two-stroke twin in 1914, followed by an excellent range of singles which were produced until the late 1930s. These stylish little motorcycles were amongst the best sellers of the day, a testimony to the designers' successful blend of reliability and economy.

Sand racing grew in popularity during the 1920s, and in England almost every suitable stretch of beach along the coast was utilised by local clubs for their meetings. Any reliable make of sports machine could be used, provided it had a foot-operated gear change lever, or one that could be knocked through with the knee, leaving both hands on the bars whilst changing down at corners where the sand was churned up. The style of riding was similar to dirt-tracking, with the cornering leg well out and forwards, where it acted as both support and skid for the broadsiding machine. Sand racing experts favoured a low, cramped-looking position, which they achieved by removing the saddle and suffering the consequences of a small cushion in its place. The long-distance races over 25 or 50 miles (40 or 80km), were more thrilling for the spectators than the sprint events, especially if the course was soft. A large number of races required a rolling start during which the riders followed a sidecar outfit at a speed of about 40mph (64kph) for half a mile or so (0.8km) until the passenger dropped his flag. Then the racers were unleashed in a neck-and-neck rush for the first bend. It was 'full-bore' all the way home after that, round and round the circuit in a cloud of flying spray, hoping not to encounter a soggy patch, dead dogfish or hole sufficiently deep to wreck a wheel. Nature was always a force to be reckoned with, especially at winter meetings, when the tide could pay a speedy and unwelcome visit to the course, washing away the marker flags and lapping the wheels o competing machines, so that both riders and bikes quickly became splattered beyond recognition. The risks involved in sand racing were not so great as on the road, because of the wide, unbroken expanse to slide about upon, and whenever a serious tumble did occur, sand was far preferable to land on than concrete. National competitions for solo and sidecar motorcycles were held on Pendine and Southport sands and attracted large crowds. Ice racing was catching on in those countries where conditions were suitable.

CT2878

LEVIS

2$\frac{1}{2}$hp Levis motorcycle, 1921

1922 1¾hp Grigg Scooter

The Reynolds Runabout for 1921

During the period of demand for cheap transport, following World War I, quite a number of firms, many of them only speculative concerns, produced scooter-like vehicles powered by a small motor. From the manufacturers' point of view they were cheap and easy to produce, having smaller wheels than a conventional motorcycle, a pressed steel or welded tube frame and a two-stroke engine. Often the designs were crude and of the stand-up-and-ride variety, with the parts clumsily arranged as seen in the illustrated Grigg's scooter, with its over-burdened rear wheel and lack of weather protection for the rider. But some of the more considered models were a brief commercial success, such as the ABC Scootamota, the two-seater Reynolds Runabout, and the fully enclosed Unibus with car-type chassis and suspension. The press and public alike thought highly of their economy. They were light, economical to run, easy to maintain, and the simple controls appealed especially to women, who otherwise might never had driven a two-wheeler. But they were vehicles for short journeys only—to the shops or for a brief spin in the country—and they never really did catch on, owing to competition from light cars.

All this motorised gadding about was a far cry from the very serious business of fast motorcycle Grand Prix racing, which was becoming an annual event in many European countries. After the Isle of Man TT, the Ulster Grand Prix was the event that appealed most to British riders, and many thousands of enthusiastic spectators carried their own machines over on the ferry too, in order to tour the delightful countryside in a leisurely fashion after watching the 205-mile race (330-km). The Belgians held their first motorcycle Grand Prix on the 188-mile Francorchamps road circuit in 1921, but high speeds were not attained until the rough, stony surface had been improved. The first two Dutch motorcycle Grands Prix took place near Assen, and were open to Dutch riders only, but in 1927 it became an international event. The German Grand Prix for motorcycles also began in 1925, using the Avus track near Berlin, and a Swiss event of this kind commenced soon afterwards. All motorcycle racing was interrupted by World War II, but the Grands Prix resumed again afterwards.

1¾hp Grigg scooter, 1922

1925 2¾hp Ner-a-Car

After a quarter century of motorcycling, it became commonplace to find the most staid-looking, family, sidecar combination propelled by a high-efficiency engine of the type that, only a few years earlier, would have raised excited comment at a race meeting. So it was not altogether surprising to find the new 1925 model of the revolutionary, all-enclosed Ner-a-Car, equipped with a 348cc OHV Blackburne engine.

Originally designed by an American, C. A. Neracher, this vehicle created quite a sensation in England when it was introduced by Sheffield Simplex, who manufactured it under licence. The long, low, pressed-steel chassis, with a huge front mudguard rigidly fixed to the frame and shielding the wheel through the whole arc of the steering lock, presented a very unconventional appearance, and the Ner-a-Car character was furthered by such features as pivot steering and long wheelbase. A low centre of gravity endowed this little two-wheeler car with superb balance and excellent steering qualities. After rigorous tests over 50 miles (80km) of rough stuff, the *Motor Cycle Magazine* reporter came to the conclusion that 'it was impossible to fall off of a Ner-a-Car', so the makers claim of 'hands off' riding at any speed between 10–50mph (16–80kph) was not so very exaggerated.

Other specifications included Sturmey Archer, three-speed gear-box with clutch and kick-starter, B and B, two-lever carburettor, chain transmission, mechanical lubrication pump, and carb-jector silencer to tone down the roar of engine exhaust. The Ner-a-Car had two internal expanding brakes on the rear wheel, one operated by foot pedal and the other by handlebar lever, as mounting a brake on the peculiar front wheel arrangement would have been extremely difficult. On a wet day, the wide, enveloping, front mudguard caught all the spray thrown up from the front tyre, whilst the side shields and partial enclosing of the rear wheel protected the riders legs. The spring frame, de luxe, all-weather model brought out in the following year, was even nearer-a-car, with a longer wheelbase, windshield, instrument board, bucket seat for the driver, and passenger sidecar. Ner-a-Car was the best of the cycle cars, but in the long run, dual identity was its downfall, as customers increasingly turned to standard motorcycles or to small motorcars.

It was excessively noisy engines that caused the loud public outcry against motorcyclists in the 1920s. Engine silencers were inefficient and were simply designed to provide the owner with a device which just satisfied the law. Legal action in England was taken by Weybridge residents, who, in spite of severe silencer regulations already imposed at Brooklands, still objected to the noise of racing motorcycles. As a result, the track was closed to motorcyclists on certain days of the week, and no event was allowed to last longer than three consecutive hours. The urgency for improved silencing was increased by the case of some two hundred or more machines passing through villages and towns at short intervals in the course of a reliability trial. Daily newspapers furthered the attack, and the police carried out a determined campaign against the owners of noisy motorcycles as well as inconsiderate drivers. Hence manufacturers were forced to pay some attention to the proper design of an engine silencer.

2¾hp Ner-a-car, 1925

1926 2¾hp AJS Motorcycle

The five Stevens brothers, sons of a Black Country engineer, started their motorcycle business in 1897. They first used the American Mitchell engine, which was designed to fit above the front down tube of an ordinary pedal bicycle, but within a few years they were able to produce 2½ and 3¼hp air and water-cooled power units themselves, and in addition supplied engines to other motorcycle and motor tricycle manufacturers. Their first machine was a compact, lightweight model with a 292cc, single-cylinder engine, two-speed countershaft gear-box and choice of belt or chain drive. It arrived on the market in 1909 and carried the trade name AJS, those being the initials of Albert John Stevens, who besides playing a leading role in the formation of the company, also used his outstanding ability as a rider to establish an early reputation for the marque in trial and racing events.

On the Isle of Man in 1914 the AJS team, riding newly designed 350cc singles, beat the rest of the field, taking first and second place in the junior race, with a winning speed only 4mph (6.4kph) slower than the winner of the senior event. Commercial production of the road-going version

of this successful racer was halted by the outbreak of war, as was the 'Ajays' promising TT career. Six years later when the machines lined up for the start again in Glencrutchery Road (Isle of Man) considerable interest was aroused by the appearance of the six-speed, 350cc AJS model with unique new engine features in the form of push-rod-operated OHVs and hemispherical cylinder head. Its performance was superb over a course which had been altered since the last event, and even though rider Cyril Williams had to push home from Craig-ny-Baa, he won the race by a clear ten minutes. In the following year's TT the 1914 winner Eric Williams led the 350cc AJS juniors into first, second and third places, whilst yet another 350cc AJS, ridden by H. R. Davies, caused a sensation by winning the senior race, beating the Indian machines ridden by Freddy Dixon and Bert Le Vack, with an average speed of 54.59mph (87.85kph). In 1922, Manx rider Tom Sheard made it four junior wins in a row for AJS.

As a result of this racing success and a fast-growing reputation for reliability on the road, the factory was able to extend its range of touring models, which were fast, delightful things to ride, with road-holding qualities that bore witness to the experience gained in TT racing.

Production at the time included a 7hp, twin-cylinder machine designed for sidecar duty. Racing man, Jimmy Simpson, was linked to AJS during the mid 1920s. Although the combination did not achieve outright TT victories, this meteoric rider created spectacular lap records of 64mph (102.9kph) in the 1924 Junior Race on a 'big-port' AJS, and then again two years later, riding a 500cc, OHV model, he brought off the first ever 70mph (112.6kph) lap in the senior event, before Stanley Woods came through to win it for Norton.

AJS were amongst those companies who changed hands during the 1930s depression. They were taken over by Collier Bros, the manufacturers of Matchless motorcycles, but continued to operate under their own name, although production was centred in London. Continental and American competitors had not been too numerous at the TT races since the early days, owing to the high entry fee and the considerable expense of sending a racing team to the Isle of Man. But the years prior to World War II saw international gatherings on the island once again. AJS produced a V-4 in 1938, with two cylinders angled forward and two back in the effort to gain advantage over Guzzi and BMW. With Walter Rusk riding it, it made the first ever 100mph (160.9kph) lap of the Ulster Grand Prix in 1939.

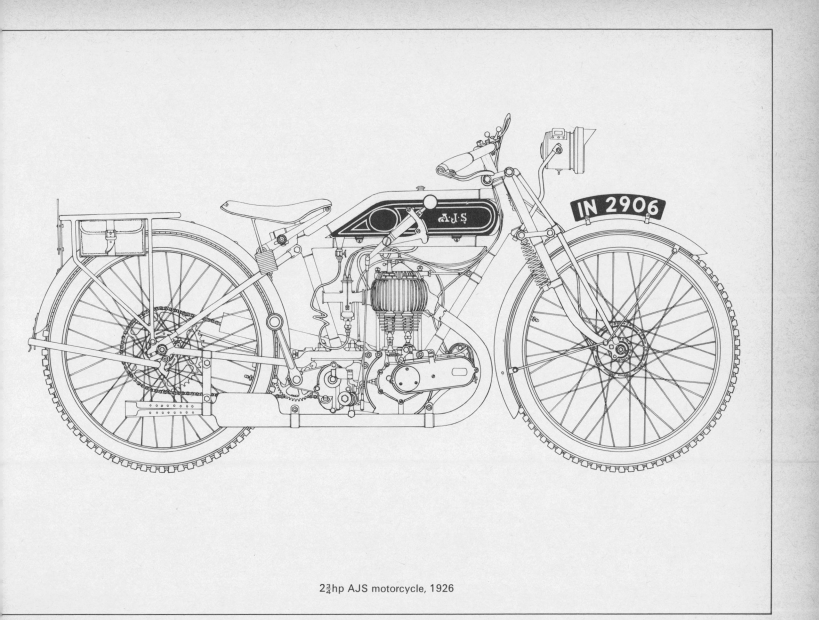

2¾hp AJS motorcycle, 1926

1928 500cc Rudge Dirt-track Motorcycle

Dirt-track or speedway racing, originated in New South Wales, Australia, during 1925 where it was first arranged as a novelty attraction at agricultural fairs. The requirements were simply a short circuit track, consisting of cinders laid on grass, which would otherwise be too slippery for the tyres, and some enthusiastic young men with stripped-down, hotted-up motorcycles, willing to risk their limbs in high-speed races against each other. The results were spectacularly successful and permanent dirt-tracks were laid, the first in 1926 at Sydney

Dual on the mountains. England versus Italy in the International TT (after the Grimes sketch for *Motorcycle*, 1927)

showground. This was the Speedway Royal, a $\frac{1}{2}$-mile (0.8-km) circuit banked to a height of 42in (106cm), and consisting of a special mixture of cinders and metal, which had to be raked flat after every race. As the speedway craze spread throughout Australia, some twenty to thirty thousand spectators were drawn to the city tracks every Saturday to see thrilling races between home-groomed stars such as Billy Lamont, and visiting Americans such as Harley Davidson expert, Eddie Brink.

Dirt-track was started in South Africa during 1927 at the Johannesburg motordrome, and New Zealand's first speedway was built soon afterwards at Monica Park, Christchurch. In 1928 two Australian promoters, Johnny S.

Hoskins and A. J. Hunting, brought a team of riders to England to establish the sport there. However, some very successful dirt-track meetings had already been held in England on a sandy $\frac{1}{4}$-mile (0.4km) circuit at Camberly Heath the previous year, when for the first time an English crowd were thrilled to see solo and sidecar events run on Australian and American lines. The only motorcycle race track in Britain at the time was Brooklands, and there was little prospect of another concrete circuit being constructed, so opinion was generally in favour of introducing this new sport, because of its cheapness as well as the thrills provided for spectators. There were those who objected however, and rumours were circulated about dreadful pile-ups, ghastly injuries and riders killed on the Australian circuits. In consequence a *Motor Cycle Magazine* correspondent wondered, 'whether the British press and public would stand for gladiatorial exhibitions of this sort', but after all, the risks involved in speed events are partly responsible for their success, and the new sport was soon well established on a professional basis. Only a few years later, at Wembley in 1936, some seventy-five thousand spectators saw Lionel Van Praag become the first dirt-track champion of the world.

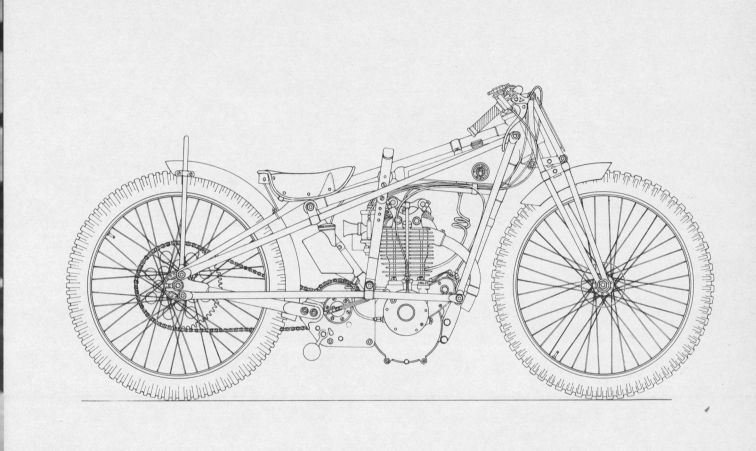

500cc Rudge dirt-track motorcycle, 1927

1928 500cc Douglas Dirt-track Motorcycle

As more riders became professional, they were able to order special dirt-track models from those manufacturers who produced a suitable engine. Harley Davidson, Scott and Rudge were high amongst the honoured, but the 500cc Douglas was pre-eminent until the era of JAP engines. The Douglas OHV, horizontally opposed engine was especially suited to dirt-track racing, and the duplex cradle frame, was designed to give ample clearance when cornering. Dual carburettors and air boxes were arranged behind fine gauze to exclude grit from the induction system, and the gear-box was a separate three-speed unit with control through levers and gate on the frame. The handlebars were styled to give maximum control of the machine at all speeds, and twist-grip control, magneto cut-out, and oil-pump lever were fitted onto the bar within easy reach of the riders' hands. Front forks had central sprung suspension and one-piece connecting links, fitted with shock absorbers and steering damper. The wheels were specially built, and the rear hub serrated on both sides so that the large sprocket could still be fitted when the wheel was reversed. Other items included, were half-guard and push-off bar over the rear wheel, foot-rest and steel knee hook, under which the rider forced his right leg to

prevent being catapulted off. His left foot was steel shod and extended out for almost the duration of the race in order to correct skids. Overtaking was chiefly done on the bends, and each lap was one gigantic broadside, with the front wheel off the track as much as on it. Broken forks and twisted frames were common, as the strain on them was simply terrific.

Douglas was certainly the most popular make of British motorcycle with the Australians, but there were some racers who preferred American machines because they had been developed on the tough, horse track circuits in the USA, and their forks, frames, and engines were thought to be more reliable. Other makes of racing bikes used on Australian tracks were Royal Enfield, New Hudson, New Imperial, BSA, Chater-Lea, Scott, Ariel, AJS, P & M, Sunbeam, Zenith, Triumph, Norton, Raleigh, and a few Indian motorcycles.

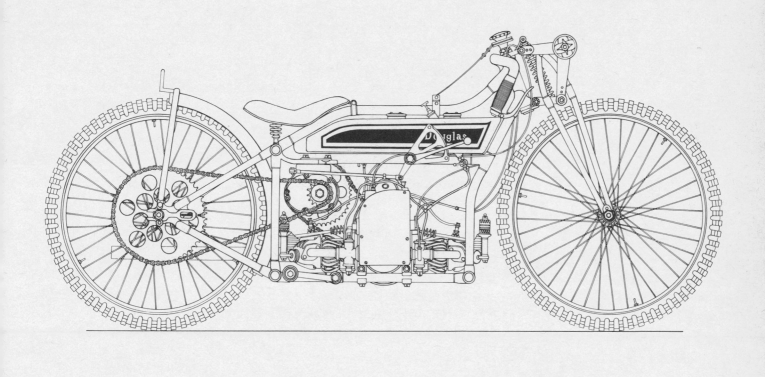

500cc Douglas dirt-track motorcycle, 1928

1929 500cc Moto Guzzi Motorcycle

The illustration shows one of the small number of continental racing motorcycles designed by Carlo Guzzi, and built especially for exclusive purchasers in England. Immediately after assembly in 1929, it was despatched from the factory at Mardello, Italy, to an English customer in Cambridge, but although it was designed to reach a top speed of about 93mph (149.6kph), there is no official evidence of it ever having been raced. After a succession of owners, the machine was restored to near-original specifications, except that the non-original, foot-operated gear control was retained. The horizontal cylinder barrel pointed forwards, so as to fully utilise the cool airstream swirling past the front wheel and, like the Rudge engine, this one also had four valves. The engine crank case and three-speed gear-box were constructed as a single unit, a sign of the then progressive times. Primary drive was through helical gears, so the engine revolved backwards. A separate oil tank with force-feed lubrication was carried above the top frame tube, a feature on many racers, and the whole machine was finished in maroon.

Moto Guzzi machines became very active on the racing scene during the twenties. In 1926 the Italian rider, Ghersi, won the lightweight TT on a Guzzi single, but was disqualified because of a spark plug irregularity. From then onwards, English domination in motorcycle sport was threatened and eventually brought to an end in 1935 when Stanley Woods won his seventh TT race on a lightweight, single-cylinder Guzzi. The same rider also won the senior TT race that year on a 500cc, V-twin Guzzi with wide-angle (120°) cylinders, at an average speed of 84mph (135.1kph) beating Jimmy Guthrie's Norton by 4sec. Guzzi thereby became the first non-English makers to win the senior TT since the Indian victory of 1911, and in addition, theirs was the first spring frame model to win a senior TT event.

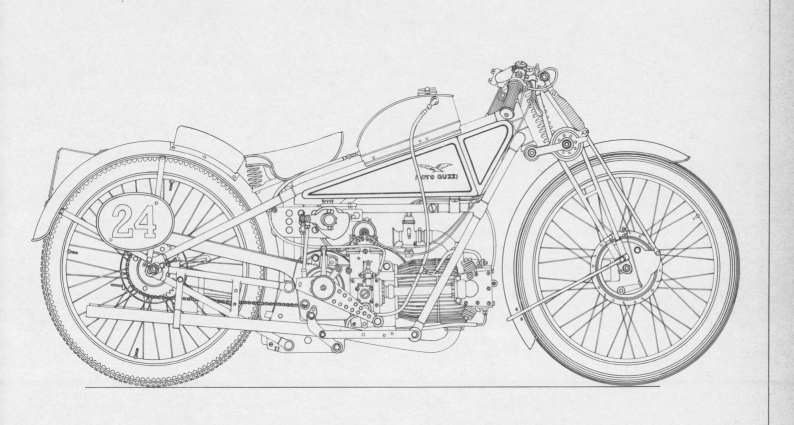

500cc Moto Guzzi motorcycle, 1929

1930 500cc Cotton-Blackburne Special Sprint Racing Motorcycle

Several manufacturers followed Scott's lead and used duplex-tubed frames in order to produce a rigid construction which did not warp under the thrust of a powerful engine, but the duplex frame was taken almost to the ultimate by Willoughby Cotton of Gloucester, England, who originally designed it for a Levis Racer in 1914–15. The illustrated Cotton motorcycle with top rails running straight from steering head to rear spindle, contained a 500cc Blackburne engine, and this combination made an extremely attractive sporting mount with a low centre of gravity and a degree of stability essential to success. The original Burman gear-box has since been modified to include a foot-change mechanism, and the alloy wheel trims and extended saddle are also more recent fitments. Besides being a streamlining feature, the latter allowed the rider to sit well back in order to prevent wheel spin and skids when getting away. Webb girder forks at the front were sheathed in alloy to lessen wind resistance, and this sprinter was equipped with only the flimsiest of brakes and the least possible number of fittings, in order to reduce its weight to the absolute minimum.

Cotton's fully triangulated, four-tubed machines with forward-inclined Blackburne and JAP engines, became famous for their racing successes, as well as acquiring a reputation for good steering and road-holding. The system resulted in an extraordinarily low riding position that was particularly favoured by sand racers, and on the Isle of Man it seemed a wonder they could ever hope to clear the humps and bridges that dotted the course. In 1923, Stanley Woods won the first of his ten Tourist Trophies on an OHV Cotton-Blackburne, and in the following decade, Francis Williams sprinted to many a victory on a machine of the same make. Motorcycle sport continued to evolve after 1930 but it became a very specialised game, with works teams monopolising the major races.

500cc Cotton-Blackburne special sprint racing motorcycle, 1930

1931 1,000cc Brough Superior Racing Combination

George Brough left his father's (W. H. Brough) firm soon after World War I, so there was no commercial or other association between the makes of Brough, and Brough Superior. George built his Superior for the 'connoisseur rider who would have the best and fastest motorcycle on the road'. He was never interested in mass-production, but instead insisted upon such high standards of design and finish that his machines became known as the 'Rolls Royce amongst motorcycles'. In 1919 he produced the first V-twin Superior motorcycle, powered by the thirsty, 90-bore Prestwich engine, which required a large-capacity, bullnosed petrol tank, the like of which has distinguished the Brough Superior ever since.

An entirely new Superior, the 1,000cc, side-valve, JAP-engined SS 80, appeared in 1923, a luxurious machine designed expressly for the solo rider, and the first side-valve model to lap the Brooklands oval at 100mph (160.9kph). The 1,000cc, overhead-valve model which followed, had already proven itself as a racer by the time it appeared on show at Olympia in 1924. Herbert Le Vack created the world's solo and sidecar records at 123mph (198kph) and

103mph (165.8kph) respectively on a SS 100. Superbly finished production models with 1,000cc capacity JAP or Anzani engines, were delivered to the customer with a guarantee of having been timed at 100mph over $\frac{1}{4}$ mile (0.4km).

Edwin Charles Ellis Baragwanath (generally shortened to Barry) began his celebrated association with Brough Superior in 1925. First as a solo rider, then as exponent of the sidecar outfit, he cracked record after record, breaking the lap record for sidecars at Brooklands in 1931 with a speed of 101mph (162.5kph), in 1932 at 103mph (165.8kph), and in 1933 at 103.97mph (167.32kph). The latter record stood for five years until broken at 106mph (170.6kph) by Noel Pope—who had by then acquired Barry's supercharged Brough Superior machine, and was riding it for the first time with the sidecar attached. No sidecar race was ever won at Brooklands with an average speed above 100mph, but in 1933 E. C. E. Baragwanath nearly pulled it off by averaging 99.22mph (159.68kph) over three laps, the fastest one at 103.37mph.

The illustration shows this successful racing combination, fitted in 1930 with a new V-twin, 1,000cc, JAP engine, incorporating a Powerplus supercharger and special car-type AMAL carburettor. Fuel consumption

proved to be at a rate of only 4mpg (less than 1.5kpl). The streamlined sidecar is simply a one-piece alloy shell with a wooden floor. Noel Pope rode the Superior again at Brooklands, but without the sidecar, in July 1939, when he established an all-time record by lapping at 124.51mph (200.38kph). The Brooklands track did not open again for racing after World War II, so the solo and sidecar lap records remain with Pope and his Brough Superior.

About the same time, Brough produced his most beautiful design— the Brough Superior Golden Dream, with a flat-four 997cc engine. This was a vast improvement over earlier four-cylinder models, but only half-a-dozen were built to special order before the factory went over to war work. Another famous exponent of Brough Superior motorcycles was Eric Fernihough, who besides establishing a record speed of 143.39mph (230.76kph) at Brooklands, also gained the world speed record with 168.8mph (271.66kph) during 1937, at Gyon in Hungary.

1,000cc Brough Superior racing combination, 1931

Acknowledgements

I would like to express my thanks to all who helped during the preparation of this book and especially to the following, who allowed me to make drawings of their vintage and veteran motorcycles, and who also provided technical information for which I am most grateful: C. E. Allen, BEM; Bert Allott; Howard Carter; W. H. Fenby; Ann and Don French; George and Len Geeson; the late John Griffith; Oliver Langton; Bryan Organ; Tony Twycross; Harley Davidson Motorcycle Co Ltd, USA; Science Museum, London; Imperial War Museum, London; Nostell Priory Motorcycle Museum, Wakefield; Motorcycle Museum, Stanford Hall, Rugby; Museum of Technology, Leicester

Bibiography

Books
Caunter, C. F. *Motor Cycles* (1956)
Clarke, R. H. *The Rolls Royce of Motorcycles* (Norwich, 1964)
Griffith, J. *Historic Racing Motorcycles* (1963)
Hough, R. & Setright, L. J. K. *A History of the World's Motorcycles* (1966)
'Ixion'. *Motor Cycle Cavalcade* (1950)
Pagé, Victor W. *Early Motor Cycles* (USA 1914)
Sheldon, J. J. *Veteran and Vintage Motorcycles* (1961)
Tragatsch, E. *The World's Motorcycles* (1964)
Wise, D. B. *Historic Motor Cycles* (1973)

Magazines
Iliffe Ltd. *The Motor Cycle Magazine* (first published 1903)

DAVID GLENN HUNT
MEMORIAL LIBRARY
GALVESTON COLLEGE